~~Notes~~ Doodles from the Margins: Three Plays
Wild Goose Dreams | Wolf Play | No More Sad Things

Copyright © 2022.
All Rights Reserved.

All the material within *Doodles from the Margins* is fully protected under the copyright laws of the United States of America, the British Commonwealth, including Canada, and all other countries of the Copyright Union. All rights, including professional and amateur stage productions, recitation, lecturing, public reading, motion picture, radio broadcasting, television and the rights of translation into foreign languages are strictly reserved.

Print edition.

ISBN: 978-1-7341402-6-2

tripwireharlot.com.

Wolf Play is reproduced by kind permission from Methuen Drama, part of Bloomsbury Publishing PLC. It was originally published in 2020 and available in a single text edition from www.bloomsbury.com.

Production History

WOLF PLAY:

Wolf Play was commissioned by Artists Repertory Theatre
Dámaso Rodriguez, Artistic Director
Sarah Horton/JS May, Managing Director
Portland, Oregon

Wolf Play was first produced as a National New Play Network Rolling World Premiere by Artists Repertory Theatre (Oregon) and Company One Theatre (Massachusetts).

Wolf Play received its New York premiere at Soho Rep.,
New York, NY
Sarah Benson, Artistic Director
Cynthia Flowers, Executive Director

Developed By Victory Gardens Theater, Chicago, Illinois
Chay Yew, Artistic Director
Erica Daniels, Managing Director
As part of IGNITION Festival of New Plays 2017

WILD GOOSE DREAMS:

Originally produced by The Public Theater
Oskar Eustis, Artistic Director
Patrick Willingham, Executive Director
in a co-production with La Jolla Playhouse
Christopher Ashley, Artistic Director
Michael S. Rosenberg, Managing Director

Wild Goose Dreams was developed by The Public Theater, the 2016 Sundance Institute Theatre Lab in MENA and at the 2016 Bay Area Playwrights Festival (Amy L. Mueller, Artistic Director). It was also created with support from the 2050 Fellowship Program at New York Theatre Workshop.

NO MORE SAD THINGS:

Co-World Premiere productions presented by Boise Contemporary Theatre, Boise, ID, and Sideshow Theatre Company, Chicago, IL.
Developed at the Lark Play Development Center, New York City

Table of Contents

Introduction 1

Author's Note 5

Wild Goose Dreams 9

Wolf Play 101

No More Sad Things 275

Acknowledgements 343

Introduction
by Sarah Ruhl

When I think of the beautiful plays in this collection by Hansol Jung, I think about these questions:

> How can we love across great distances?
>
> Are we all in a state of perpetual mourning for our contemporary loneliness?

In *No More Sad Things*, a woman goes to Maui to forget the heartbreak of her dying mother on the mainland, and she ends up falling for a local Hawaiian boy who is way too young for her. The two appeared to have met previously in a dream. We learn that this woman also terminated a pregnancy when she was the same age as the boy—in some quantum dream state, we wonder, are they the same person?

In *Wolf Play*, an American queer couple adopts a Korean boy on the internet, from another American couple who finds the boy too hard to raise, they want to "give him back." After the first adoptive parents have second thoughts, and report that the second adoptive parents are a queer family, both couples end up losing the boy to the court system.

In *Wild Goose Play*, a man, Minsung, stays in South Korea, sending all the money he earns to his family in America. (The term "Goose Fathers" literally refers to South Korean men who stay home and send their money to families in America.) Meanwhile, Minsung has an affair with a North Korean woman who is trying to defect, and she desperately misses her own father across the border and returns. Minsung is quite literally dying of loneliness.

All of these characters are trying to love across chasms, whether great spiritual distances, or national borders. These three plays comprise an extraordinary body of work by a playwright who is formally ground-breaking, profoundly insightful, full of deep-feeling, and poetically nimble. Oh—and funny.

When I first met Hansol Jung, she was a graduate student at Yale School of Drama where I teach. I remember reading her extraordinary play *Cardboard Piano*, about a forbidden relationship between the daughter of an American missionary and a Ugandan woman. And I thought—my God, how is Hansol writing so outside of her own experience, it's remarkable. As I got to know Hansol better, I learned that she grew up in Korea but also in Africa as the daughter of a pastor.

Hansol's plays all upset the narrative of what we think we might know about a person. Her characters' lives are always more complicated than what meets the eye.

For example, in *Wolf Play*, a Wolf begins by telling us:

> "What if I said I am not what you think you see.
>
> I am not an actor human, this floor is forest earth, and to the left of that glaring exit light, a river flows, the width and length and velocity of the Egyptian Nile.
>
> The truth is a wobbly thing, we shall wobble through our own set of truths like jello on a freight train, and tonight I add a bump to that journey and put to you my truth:
> I am not what you think you see.
> I am the wolf.
>
> Aow.
> yes, I am the wolf.
> Aooow.
> And then again because three translates to God in bible, infinity in Asia, and funny in theater: I am the wolf."

In all three plays, a story-teller grabs the hand of the audience and leads us through the mythic and poetic terrain we are about to enter, creating intimacy with the audience, and shattering the fourth wall and its expectations of realism. In *Wolf Play*, this guide is a wolf. In *No More Sad Things*, our guide is, funnily enough, a guidebook to Maui. In *Wild Goose Dream*, our guide is a digital Greek chorus.

These guides allow us into a netherworld where our hearts might get broken. Our hearts are broken in *Wolf Play* when the chosen family we have come to love loses their boy to the court system because of homophobic adoption laws. Our hearts are also broken when Minsung, in *Wild Goose Dreams*, commits suicide, and his daughter, never having really known him, comes to his funeral, and then keeps leaving messages on his answering machine, saying, "I didn't really know you....So I am sorry. But now I have to be sorry forever."

Hansol continually breaks our hearts, but also continually breaks up this suffering with humor, as in the title *No More Sad Things,* which is the protagonist's mantra. Jessiee, our heroine, is continually breaking off her speech in the middle, saying "No more sad things." Suffering in all three plays is both softened and deepened by myth. Looking up at the constellations on the ceiling, the young pregnant Jessiee says, "You can't expect me to give up my life for a myth."

The myth in question is Callisto. In Jung's world, bears and beasts and geese and wolves have their way with us, even when we think we are modern people with digital armor. The millennial world bleeds into the ancient world and back again. Nations bleed into other nations. Dreams bleed into other dreams.

The alienation of being separate, connected only through the digital world causes one character in *Wild Goose Dreams* to say, "I wish you were more real for me. I wish I were more real for you." Minsung at first asks Nanhee, "Why are You on this website?" And she answers quite simply, "I got a free trial in my inbox. But mostly because I am lonely too."

"Mostly because I am lonely too." This straightforward cry of the heart leaps out from all of these plays. These works of art are tender, and also spiky—hungry for connection and transcendence. This longing for authentic human love persists in all of these plays, over and above the noise of the dehumanizing capitalist world—a world in which a baby can be traded on the internet, and a man can become nothing more than his wallet.

In *Wild Goose Dreams,* one character asks: "What are you doing for Christmas?"

And the chorus answers:

> "Do things! Buy things! Look at all these other people who are happier than you!"

These plays all seem to ask how can we do differently? Must we spend our lives buying things, and examining the apparently happier lives of others who we only dimly apprehend?

There are more questions in these plays than answers, which make them my kind of favorite play. That Hansol has chosen to doodle in these margins, to write into and onto her plays, is a formal testament to her desire for messiness over resolution. The hope is that what was in the margins becomes central. I'll leave you with the last speech from *Wolf Play:*

> What if I said
> I am not what you think you see.
> I am not human, this floor is forest earth, and to the left of that glaring exit light, a river flows,
> You are not what you feel you are, you are a spider, an eagle
> Or a wolf.
> What if I said you are a wolf?
> What if I said you are the single most important breath in my space. You are the first gear that turns the clock of my world. What if I said I will fight for you with every blood cell and cranial nerve I possess. And you believed me? Does that change anything?"

Author's Note

I was never a doodler.
I have, in fact, a real fear of it.
Putting things down on print,
It is so permanently judgeable, no?
I experience something akin to
STAGE FRIGHT when a play goes to
print after Final Proof.
"wait wait no there might be more
   things I learn, more things to change!"
And so this experiment of
putting more permanent marks
on a permanently printed anthology
is likely to backfire for us —
For me, a wince-worthy document
recording a historic hansol who thought
this would be a fun gag
For you, an annoying read.

But I hate to admit
that I was ever wrong
And so I went through with
the historic hansol's idea.
So here are my doodles.
Some are personal thoughts,
most are odd drawings,
A few valuable gift doodles
From those I call my family.

A play is never finished.

Not the writing of it,
Not the reading of it,
And hopefully never the
endless ways to journey through it.
I hope your journeys are
ones that touch your hearts.
            Love, Hansol
      Mystic CT, August 8, 202

Wild Goose Dreams

A gift doodle from the infinite heart of Leigh Silverman

CHARACTERS

GUK MINSUNG	South Korean man, early forties.
YOO NANHEE	North Korean woman, late thirties
FATHER	North Korean man, late fifties. Nanhee's father.
CHORUS	a chorus of voices, as many as possible.
- MAN	part of chorus / the digital Minsung
- WOMAN	part of chorus / the digital Nanhee
- HEEJIN	part of chorus / Minsung's daughter
- WIFE	part of chorus / Minsung's wife

SETTING

Seoul, South Korea. Now ish

PUNCTUATION NOTES

-    a cut off either by self or other.
/   a point where another character might cut in.
[words] that are thought but unspoken.

Right Alignment
happens when speaker is in another reality

which is different from the speaker with lines in
Left Alignment

Center Alignment
happens when speakers in different realities
speak the same lines simultaneously

For CHORUS:
unbulleted chorus lines are spoken by all chorus members.

- Bulleted chorus lines are spoken by one chorus member

<u>Bold Underlined</u> chorus lines cues a shift in binary codes

1   is pronounced one
0   is pronounced zero

And when **1** or **0** is **BOLDED** it is being sung in beautiful and impossible harmonies, a cappella.

[one] *This monologue is forever indebted to the great performance of Francis Jue*

FATHER

Once upon a time there was an angel.
She lived in the heavens with all the other angels.
One day some of them decide to defy the Heavenly Emperor and sneak down to earth. Sneak sneak sneak.
They find an earthly river, fling off their heavenly robes and jump in, they're just chilling, having some earthly fun... and a woodcutter passes by, hears heavenly noises and sneaks up to the river sneak sneak sneak! What does he see? Naked angels. He is so surprised, backs up, and slips on a pile of heavenly robes. Woah. They are so beautiful and so strange he cannot help but take one. Then he creeps off. Creep creep creep.
Sun sets, the angels are exhausted, "Arh! I'm exhausted," they say, "yeah yeah let's get outta here, let's go grab a heavenly beverage," they dry up and get ready to fly back home except this one angel, "Where are my clothes!" She exclaims, because they can't fly back without their clothes, it's like their wings? Her angel friends feel so bad, but what can they do? So they say sorry and goodbye.
And the lonely angel stays in the river, cold, hungry and very angry.
Next day, the woodcutter returns to find the angel girl, still cold, hungry and very angry. He says, "please angel come to my home. I make some really good seaweed soup." Angel girl thinks, food. Mmmmm FOOD. And all of her cold and anger? It is gone for a time.
They have the yummy soup, she gets earthly clothes, they fall in love get married have lots of angel-human babies, babies grow up and go off to college, and they are growing old together.
Then one day, the once-angel finds her heavenly robes hidden under the floorboards of her house. Panicked and scared, Woodcutter cuts in, "No no I can explain." And he does, and he cries, and she cries, and they share a renewed love that had gotten stale after years of domestic stasis. And then she puts on the robes. Woodcutter is so surprised he says, "But what about our family? Our love? You are my wife!" Angel girl says, "Fuck you. I can fly." And then she disappears into the heavens never to return.

If you have to choose between family and flying,
I hope you would choose the flying.
And don't tell mommy I said that.
Also don't tell mommy I said fuck you.

Okay. Time for bed. Everyone go to sleep now.

[two]

CHORUS

- Please restart your system to install important updates. Voooooooooooooooong~ Bum!
- LOVE THIS!
- Like.
- LOVE THIS!
- Like.
- This kitten.
- This puppy!

THIS.

- Breaking News! Presidential summit at the DMZ cancelled due to
- POP UP Win a free trip to the paradise of your dreams
- Ding! from calendar. Traffic is slower than usual leave now for / meeting with
- POP UP you know you deserve this special
- Close. Look up: traffic in Seoul, Search.
- *(sung)* 010/01 01 01 001 01, [*spoken simultaneously:* Searching (x4)]
- There are about 203,000 results for traffic in Seoul
- Ding Dong! Fine dust alert, / do not leave your
- Delete
- *(sung)* 1011/00101 [*spoken simultaneously:* Deleting]
- Deleted
- Look up: cheap flights to Connecticut, Search
- *(sung)* 010/01 01 [*spoken simultaneously:* Searching (x2)]
- There are about / 45,000 results
- Breaking News! Presidential Summit still happening according to
- Delete
- *(sung)* 1011 / 00101
- Deleting
- What's on Your Mind?
- What's on Your Mind?
- What's on Your 1011

MAN	CHORUS	WOMAN	CHORUS
	10111		- What's on your mind? What's on your mind?
	001010	scroll	
scroll	011001		
scroll	11101		
	00111		- Ding! from Calendar Traffic is slower than usual. Leave now for meeting with / **101100101**
	001001		
	11001	**Delete**	

MAN	CHORUS	WOMAN	CHORUS
scroll			- POP UP Breaking News! Missile tests resume from the North.
	- What's on your / mind? What's on your mind? What's on your mind	**Go to** **Link**	
Escape		**Escape**	**101100** **10110/**
			- Ding! from Calendar Traffic is slower than
Delete	- POP UP Breaking/ **101100101**	**Delete**	
Look up: Chicken and beer delivery,			**101100101**
Search			- Ding! from Calendar/
	01 001		**101100**
Search		**Delete**	
Search	- Loading	**Delete**	**10** Ding!
Search	- Loading	**Delete**	**10** Ding!
Refresh	**01001**	**Delete**	
			10 Ding!
Search		**Delete**	
Search		**Delete!**	Dingdingdingding

CHORUS

No response

MAN

Search

WOMAN

Escape

CHORUS

No response

MAN & WOMAN

Close.

CHORUS

-System not responding.

MAN & WOMAN

Reboot.

CHORUS

Voooooooooooooooong~ Bum!
-Katok Katok!

WOMAN

Your have one new Talk from Song Ji Ah.

*Dear Reader, please feel free to read "poke" as whatever relevant verb your chosen social media platform has dictatated for you.

Do people still poke!?

CHORUS

-Nanhee, it's Ji Ah. Here's the number for my broker. He goes by Mister Lee. Not cheap but worth it.

MAN

Poke Heejin Cook. You have successfully poked Heejin Cook.
Minsung, what's on your mind?

WOMAN

Nanhee, what's on your mind?

CHORUS

Brinng Brinng
Brinng Brinng
Brinng Brinng
Brinng
 - The account you are trying to reach is currently unavailable.
   Please try again after the
Peeeeeeeeeeeeeeeeep

NANHEE

Mister Lee, hello. This is Yoo Nanhee
I got your number from my friend Song Ji Ah,
she said you were able to connect her to her family in the North.
I too have family in North Korea,
I defected about four years ago.
And I want to smuggle a phone to them as well.
If you can help, please call me at this number.
Again, my name is Yoo Nanhee.
Thank you.

CHORUS

Brinng Peeeeeeeeeeeeeeeeep

MINSUNG

Hello from Seoul, it's me, Minsung.
I'm alone at the office.
I called our daughter but she is not picking up,
so,
I am calling the wife.
Hi wife.
Seven years and I still can't get the time difference right.
Sorry.
Anyway.
Call me when you can.
I'll be here all night.
Be well.

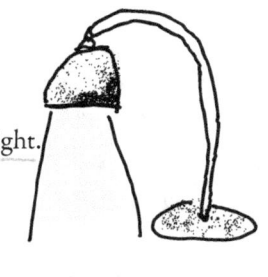

CHORUS

- Disconnected.

MAN

Open email

CHORUS

- No new emails.

WOMAN

Open messages

CHORUS

- No new messages.

MAN & WOMAN

Open Facebook

CHORUS

-No new Facebook notifications.

MAN

Scroll

WOMAN

Scroll

CHORUS

-twenty eight reasons skinny is the new fat
-Twenty one images of humanity
-epic fails
-the best no make up look with make up

WOMAN

Save

CHORUS

-Why Footloose was the Frozen of the 80s
-*(sung)* ***I need a hero I'm holding out for a***
-Loneliness is the true cause of addiction

MAN

Escape

CHORUS

- More senior citizens living alone in Seoul than ever before

WOMAN

Escape

CHORUS

-*(sung)* ***Lonely Lonely Lonely Lonely Lonely, Baby I'm so Lonely***
-Depressed? Lonely? Sad? Join us at Praise on Wednesdays dot Onnuri Church dot

MAN & WOMAN

Escape.

CHORUS

-No new Facebook notifications
-No new messages

WOMAN

Open Tetris

MAN

Open Angry Birds

Gaming sounds from chrous
(via amazing and virtuosic a cappella)

CHORUS

-*(Kakaotalk notification)* Katok! Katok!

WOMAN

You have one new Talk from Love Genie.

CHORUS

(Love Genie Jingle, sung) Ah~~

WOMAN
Congratulations, Yoo Nanhee!
You've been selected for a one month free trial membership at
Love Genie dot Co dot Kr.
Thousands of elite men are just waiting for your poke of love.
Join now!

CHORUS
(*Love Genie Jingle, sung*) Ah~~

MAN
Welcome back, MrGooseMan! You have no new messages

WOMAN
Are you sure you would like to delete this talk?

CHORUS
(*sung*) **1011 00101**

WOMAN
Talk deleted.

MAN
Scroll

WOMAN
Scroll

CHORUS
-Ping! Newsletter from Nature. Penguin Factoids. Click / here to unsubscribe
-POP UP Seven reasons why reunification will benefit both / Koreas
-Breaking News! / Terror!
-What's on your mind?
-What's /on your mind? What's on your 1011 What's on your 1011 What's on your 1011
-Ding! from /calendar
-POP UP remember me?

CHORUS
Brinng Brinng
Brinng Brinng
Brinng Brinng
   - Connecting.

MINSUNG
Heejin? How are you? How is America? How is school? Sad? Why? What? Why are you sad about an A minus in World History?

NANHEE
Hello? Father?
It's me. Nanhee. Your daughter.
Can you hear me? Hello?
Yes it's really me. I didn't drown in the river. I am alive, in the south.

MINSUNG
Don't be sad, it's okay! You are my daughter. You are a genius.

NANHEE
What? I can't hear you very well.

MINSUNG
Genius. You don't know that word? In English it is **big head**. **Big Einstein head**.
Daddy have Einstein head, Daughter have Einstein head, understand?
It is extra? I don't know what–
Ah. Heejin. That is not very respectful of your father

NANHEE
Are you crying? Please don't cry father,
I am very alive and very successful.
I have sent you money through the broker,
Mister Lee, who gave you the phone. Did you get it?

MINSUNG
A boyfriend?

NANHEE
What? I think the connection is very bad, there is a lot of static noise - can you speak louder? Hello?

MINSUNG
Heejin, could you slow down please daddy is not so good at English.
Boyfriend yes? Boyfriend no?

NANHEE
Oh! Yes of course I have a husband, and children.

---

[1] Bolded bits in Minsung's lines are spoken with a thick Korean accent.

MINSUNG
Heejin, show daddy **Boyfriend photograph**

NANHEE
Sons. Two sons. I have two children who are male and
I am very happy and very successful.

MINSUNG
Oh. **Burrito.** I thought you said **Boyfriend.**
Well, send a picture when you have one, okay?
Or you could friend me on facebook? I have applied to be your friend
Why? I can friend. Daddy will good friend.
C'mon. It'll be fun.
Yes?!

NANHEE
Yes I am happy. Of course I am happy.
I never thought I would hear your voice ever again, and there you are.
I am sorry, for everything.

MINSUNG
Already? My daughter is the busiest girl in Fairfield Connecticut.

MINSUNG & NANHEE
Be healthy, okay?

CHORUS
-Disconnected

NANHEE
Hello?
...
Open trash.

CHORUS
(*Love Genie Jingle, sung*) **Ah~~**

WOMAN
Congratulations, Yoo Nanhee!
You've been selected for a one month free trial membership at Love
Genie dot co dot kr. Thousands of elite men are just waiting for your
poke of love.
Join now!

NANHEE
Join.

MAN
Minsung, What's on your Mind?

MINSUNG
View friends.

MAN
You have 9 friends.

WOMAN
Enter username to create your new profile

MAN
Guk Minsung sent Heejin Cook a friend request.

NANHEE
QueenNanhee

WOMAN
is already in use

MINSUNG

NANHEE
NanheeIsPretty

WOMAN
is already in use

MINSUNG

MAN
You have already sent a request to Heejin Cook.

NANHEE
NanheeIsPretty81

WOMAN
is already in use

MINSUNG

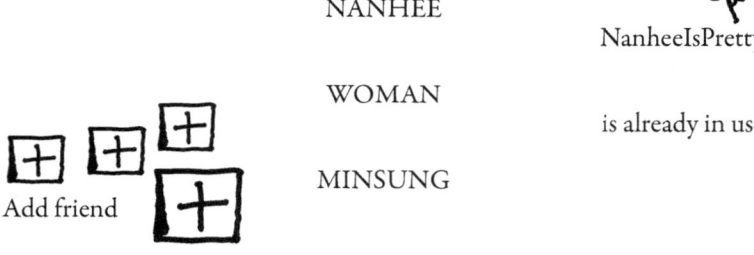

CHORUS
(*Love Genie Jingle, sung*) *Ah~~*

MAN
Welcome back, MrGooseMan

NANHEE
MinersDaughter

[handwritten margin note: This was our audition side for "WOMAN"... writers are cruel Actors are awesome.]

WOMAN
is available. Would you like to claim it?

MAN
You have no new messages.

[handwritten margin note: Can you imagine coming in at 10AM to say this like you believe it?]

WOMAN
Congratulations, MinersDaughter!

CHORUS
-Welcome!
-to the land of *(sung)* ***love*** where you will finally meet that person of your dreams.
-Click here to browse your matches

WOMAN
We have found 25 new matches! Would you like to send a love poke?
Message from MinersDaughter,

NANHEE
Hello you look very nice I love your eyes.
Would you like to create grandsons for my father just kidding.
Say hello back if you like stupid jokes such as above!

WOMAN
Sent to PrettyBoy123, Select All Copy Paste
Hello you look very nice I love your eyes.
Would you like to blahdiblahdiblah such as above!
Sent to JustANormalDudeISwear, Copy Paste Hello you look very etc
Sent to Iamthefifthbeatle Copy Paste Hello you etc, Sent to
DumpsterFireZZZ Sent to -
Retrieve message to DumpsterFireZZZ.
Sent to / MrGooseMan

MAN
MrGooseMan! You have 1 new message.
Would you like to reply to MinersDaughter?

23

MAN (cont)
Hello back. You look very nice too. Do you like karaoke? Sent to

MAN & WOMAN
MinersDaughter

WOMAN
You have 1 new message. Would you like to reply to -
I've never been to karaoke.
Send.

MAN
You've never been to Karaoke never ever? That's crazy! Smiling Crying Face.
Send.

WOMAN
Why?
Send.

MAN
I don't know anyone who's never been to karaoke before! Surprised Face
with Hands on Cheeks
Send.

LOVED watching Julian Cihi doing these ENTER like he was the Calvin Klein underwear model... ♡

WOMAN
I'm from North Korea. Defector.
Send.

MAN
Oh wow.
Send.

WOMAN
Is that weird?
Send

MAN
No! I love North Korea I've always wanted to go to- Delete.
How are you liking capitalism? Is it very di!erent than- Delete.
What the hell am I supposed to say to that of course it's weird delete delete

(PANIC) !!

WOMAN
?
Send.

MAN
I'm married.
Send.

(PANIC) X 1000001011...

Not sure why but it always made me so happy to hear this part out loud.

WOMAN
...?
Send.

Is that a joke? Send.
Sometimes I don't get South Korean jokes. Send.

MAN
Yes. It's a joke, a South Korean joke, you wouldn't understand because Delete delete delete.
No. Not a joke. Send.

WOMAN
I guess no grandsons for my father. Send.

MAN
Not from me, as far as- Delete.
LOL. Send.

WOMAN
Why are you on this website? Send.

MAN & MINSUNG
I'm lonely.

WOMAN & NANHEE
Oh.

NANHEE
" at makes me sad.

MINSUNG
Me too. Why are You on this website?

NANHEE
I got a free trial in my inbox.
But mostly because I am lonely too.

MINSUNG
So. Karaoke? Maybe?

NANHEE
Probably not a good Delete.

ESC

25

WOMAN
As friends? Smiley face. Send.

MAN
Of course!! umbs up thumbs up smiley face. Send.

Chorus erupt into individual renditions of Noraebang singing!!!

> This page is dedicated to all the actors! who throughout the (very long) development of this play humored me with their favorite / most hated Karaoke Cliché

[three]

Minsung and Nanhee are in a bed.

Father sits somewhere nearby

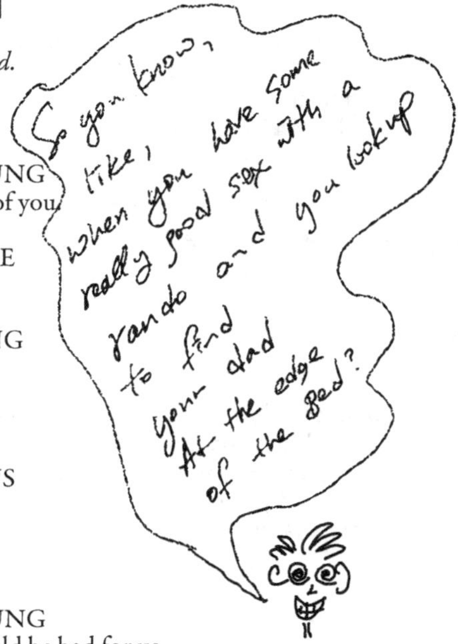
So you know, like, when you have some really good sex with a rando and you look up to find your dad At the edge of the bed?

MINSUNG
I am a responsible man. I will take care of you.

NANHEE
Thank you.

MINSUNG
And the baby. If there is a baby.

Minsung plays with his phone

CHORUS
-No new emails
-No new messages
-No new facebook notifications

MINSUNG
But I could never get a divorce that would be bad for us,

NANHEE
Mhm

MINSUNG
because this is an affair

Real thing said to me by Real one night stand. Sir, I do not remember your name nor much else about this night but THANK you for the **INSPIRATION**

CHORUS
-Search: Husband affair asset division.
-Askkorealaw dot com Q&A
-Q. My dirty husband is sexing with our daughter's tutor. Will I get rich if I divorce him or should I make him suffer?
-A. Make him suffer.

PANIC

MINSUNG
Although, my wife and daughter have been in America for seven years, I don't think they'd know if I lit myself on fire, how will they know that I'm having an affair? They call us the goose fathers, I could look that up for you.

CHORUS

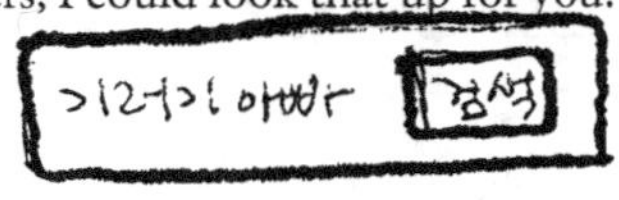
기러기 아빠
검색

-Search: Goose father origin
-Wikipedia Korea

MINSUNG
Aha.

CHORUS
—The goose father is a Korean man who works in Korea while his wife and children stay in an English-speaking country for the sake of the children's education. / The term is

MINSUNG
The term is inspired by the fact that geese migrate, just as the goose dad must travel a great distance to see his family.

NANHEE
That's nice.

MINSUNG
I'm just babbling on like the energizer bunny blablablablablah. Sorry. Ah. That is probably not what you want to hear. I know women do not like to hear it when a man apologizes. Especially after. Maybe before is okay. During is terrible. Or is it sexy? Is it sexy to apologize during sex in North Korea? Nanhee, is it sexy to apologize during sex in North Korea?

NANHEE
It depends on the North Korean you are apologizing to.

MINSUNG
Oh. Are you angry with me?

NANHEE
No.

MINSUNG
You look angry. Or sad. Or faraway. Like you are unsatisfied with me. Was it not good? Did you not like the sex we had?

NANHEE
My father is here.

MINSUNG
Hm?!

NANHEE
My father. He is here.

MINSUNG
Your father? Where?

NANHEE
There. He appeared when you first entered.

MINSUNG
When I entered?

NANHEE
Me.

MINSUNG
Oh. Is that a joke? A North Korean joke?

NANHEE
No.

MINSUNG
Did it help your sex to see him?

NANHEE
No.

MINSUNG
Have you dealt with your guilt?

NANHEE
Excuse me?

MINSUNG
I looked up North Korean defectors. On Youtube? I was preparing for our date.

Father grunts, like he is annoyed.
He leaves. To the bathroom.
Nanhee follows him to the bathroom.

MINSUNG (cont)
Many people were having problems of guilt. Maybe government brainwashing has made you feel guilty about leaving your fatherland-, I'm sorry that was a stupid thing to say

The bathroom door is locked.

NANHEE
It's locked.

[handwritten margin note: Real Question Hansol asked Mr. One Night Stand (said) i don't remember the answer]

MINSUNG
Maybe I locked it by mistake. I used it after we- Did you need to go?

Sound of pee hitting the water in toilet bowl.

NANHEE

Oh!

MINSUNG

What?

NANHEE

He's peeing.

MINSUNG

Should I leave?

NANHEE

This is your place.

MINSUNG

It's not.

NANHEE
Did we drunkenly walk into somebody else's place?

MINSUNG
No, we drunkenly walked into a motel.

NANHEE

You said this was your place.

MINSUNG

I think I drunkenly lied.

NANHEE

Why?

MINSUNG
I don't know. I wanted to impress you.

peeing stops for a bit.

NANHEE
Oh. That is nice.
Is that how South Korean men impress women, take them to a motel?

MINSUNG
If they live in a *koshiwon*, motels seem the better option

flushing sound. other noisy sounds from bathroom continue.

MINSUNG
A *koshiwon* is a small room for students who are preparing for exams. The bed folds out from the wall and the shower head hangs directly over the toilet bowl.

NANHEE
I know what a *koshiwon* is. Are you preparing for exams?

MINSUNG
No, it is the most cheap and convenient housing. I have a very good salary, but I am sending it all to my family in another country.

NANHEE
Me too. Only, I can't be sure that they actually get what I send.

Gunshot from bathroom mid-bathroom sou **BANG**

NANHEE
(sound of sharp surprise and fear)

MINSUNG
What? What's wrong?

Nanhee opens bathroom, it's no longer locked. She runs in.

MINSUNG
Are you angry with me? I can still take care of you, I have enough for that. But. I cannot get a divorce. That is my limit. My only limit. No divorce.

Nanhee returns. Father is back in room somewhere. Maybe on bed.

Leigh gave me such a nice compliment for my 110th rewrite of this father entry line.

FATHER
He is not very good looking for a South Korean Man.

MINSUNG
I'm sorry but it is for my daughter, I cannot free myself from my daughter.

!!PLAYWRIGHTS WHO COMPLIMENT THEIR DIRECTORS HOORAY!!

FATHER

That's a lot of baggage to take on for a not good looking South Korean Man.

MINSUNG

You look worried.

FATHER

You do. Is it me or is it him.

NANHEE

I want to leave.

MINSUNG

Now?

NANHEE

Where is my bra.

MINSUNG

Did I say something wrong?

NANHEE

I can't find my bra.

MINSUNG

Is it because of the divorce? The no divorce rule?

I can never read this scene without hearing Sandra Oh's MEZZO Alto voice Yelling the word BRA! BRA! Like its the thing that will glue Nanhee's sanity back together

FATHER

I think I saw him hide it.

NANHEE

Did you hide my bra?

MINSUNG

What? hide? I didn't hide

NANHEE

Keep it.

#CALLBACK

FATHER

Maybe he hid it under the floorboards so you can't fly away? Like the angel and the woodcutter!

NANHEE

I don't need my bra to fly away.

MINSUNG

Okay?

FATHER
I know you don't sweetie, it was a metaphor.

MINSUNG
Hey. Nanhee. What is going on.

NANHEE
I spoke with my father the other day.

*Goose Prompt #1
When you need to boil out of a chaotic scene make the character speak the truth in as few words as possible

FATHER
First time in four years.

MINSUNG
I thought your family was still on the other side.

FATHER
        We are.

NANHEE
They are. We smuggled a phone.

FATHER
        She did.

MINSUNG
A phone? You can do that?

NANHEE
I guess so.

FATHER
      And I wept with joy!
      Through tears I said,
I can't believe you are alive are you married do you have children
          and are they male!

NANHEE
But I, um, lied about having sons.

MINSUNG
...sons?

NANHEE
He was crying, I was feeling, feelings, and I wanted him to know I was okay. So I said I have two sons and a husband and then looked for potential husband and two sons on the internet.

MINSUNG
Oh.

FATHER
But then she found you.

MINSUNG
So you think he appeared to say no don't do that,

FATHER
I didn't say anything like that.

MINSUNG
like your conscience?

FATHER
I just watched and then said he was a not good looking man with a lot of baggage.

MINSUNG
He came to say, it's okay I don't need you to find babies on the internet?

FATHER
Don't listen to him I want the babies.

NANHEE
Shut up! Just everyone, sht.

MINSUNG & FATHER
Oh. Sorry.

NANHEE
I'm, leaving.

MINSUNG
Okay let's go.

FATHER
About time.

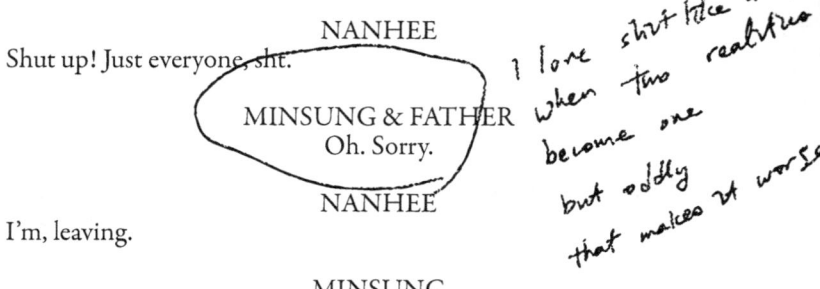
I love shit like this when two realities become one but oddly that makes it worse

NANHEE
No! You, stay.

MINSUNG
This really is not my apartment.

FATHER
I don't want to stay. I don't know that guy.

MINSUNG
Um wait Nanhee

NANHEE
What?

MINSUNG
Just, here's my card, if you need anything at all

NANHEE
Keep the card. Keep the bra. Keep everything. Thank you. Thank you for the sex. Goodbye.

She's gone.

MINSUNG
Oh.

Minsung's phone rings.

CHORUS
brinng brinng
brinng brinng
brinng brinng

Minsung checks caller ID.

CHORUS
brinng brinng
brinng brinng
brinng

MINSUNG
Hello wife.
Oh thank you. Yes I did something special for my birthday.
Oh. That's okay. We're too old for birthday presents, anyway.
Yes. The salary is slim this month.

MINSUNG (cont)
No I am not drinking away the money. The company withheld -
Oh. I didn't know it was a joke.
Haha.
Already? Okay. Thanks for calling.
Be well. I miss

CHORUS

-Disconnected

MINSUNG

you.

MAN

Compose new email.
To: Wife.

MINSUNG

Dear Wifey
For my birthday I wish for you to miss me.
I wish to be more than an ATM machine that needs to be called at times such as birthdays. Haha.
I wish for you to flirt with me, cry for me, send me care packages with thick socks and those terrible American snacks, like you used to do
I wish I knew how you taste now.
I wish I knew when you are joking or not.
I wish you were more real for me.
I wish I were more real for you.

MAN

Are you sure you'd like to close the browser?
Save or Discard draft?

MINSUNG

Discard

He crawls back into bed with a certain sadness.
And comes back up with a bra.
Smells it.
It's nice.

This vignette sequence was really hard to get right... [four] *(Good luck directors!) ... and thank you.*

CHORUS
-Minersdaughter, it's been a whole week since your very first Genie date! Tell us all about it and receive another free month of membership.
-Katok! Katok! 카톡!
-Nanhee, it's Ji Ah. How did it work out with the broker Mister Lee?
-Dear Miss Yoo, office is out of coffee and orange juice. Would you take care of that asap?

                         FATHER
                                    It's very interesting, your life.

                         NANHEE
                                                Thank you.

                         FATHER
Is that your whole job? Stocking beverages for the office workers of the
                                    South Korean Government?

                         NANHEE
                                                Of course not.
I'm just, in the process of climbing the social ladder of capitalism.

                         FATHER
                                       Very impressive.

                         NANHEE
                                              Thank you.
Are you saying that because my mind wants you to say that or because you
           are really saying that? Because you aren't really my father,
                  just the father that as been created by my mind, right?
                                      Am I going crazy?

                         FATHER
                                   That's okay sweetie.
       Sometimes a broken mind is the only way to find comfort.
        Come on. Let's go find some coffee and orange juice.

Hooray!!

                         NANHEE
                                 We do it on the internet.

                         HEEJIN
Heejin Cook accepted your friend request. Write on Heejin's Wall.

MAN
Hello daughter! I am so happy we are friends! Do you have a boyfriend yet?

HEEJIN
Message from Heejin Cook,
Hiya pops! Fyi no stuff on the wall, just pm me if u wanna chat, k?

MAN
What is pm?

Huge Thanks to SAMANTHA WANG of the La Jolla cast. In the coinage of Heejin's language use —

HEEJIN
OMG you are so extra,
just write wot u wanna say in the space below this msg.

MAN
MSG? Like the ingredient?

HEEJIN
LMAO no sorry, I meant message. But you did it right you sent that last one as a msg.

MAN
Smiley face with bulging hearts for eyes thumbs up thumbs up

HEEJIN
Smiley face with bulging hearts for eyes thumbs up thumbs up
Ima go delete ur wallposts, k?

FATHER
Let's go out tonight! Call all your friends! I want to meet them.

NANHEE
How?

FATHER
A one-way meeting. Aren't you curious what I think of your rich flashy South Korean friends?

NANHEE
I don't have any.

For the longest time Having friends felt like the biggest measure of success re: my immigration process in USA ..... Is that what

FATHER
Really?

NANHEE
What?

38

FATHER
It's just so unlike you, to have no friends.

CHORUS
(*Love Genie Jingle, sung*) *Ah~*

WOMAN
MrGooseMan has logged in

FATHER
Well, you have that guy.

NANHEE
I do have that guy.

MAN
Message from MrGooseMan, Hello lady!

WOMAN
Hi.

MAN
We should go out again. I have something that belongs to you.
Smiley devil face.

FATHER
He kept your bra. Winner.

NANHEE
Don't be so judge-y.
I'm over thirty and haven't had plastic surgery.
I'm surprised he's still talking to me two weeks after sex.

MAN
Wanna go Karaoke again?

WOMAN
It was very loud. Monkey with hands over ears.

[handwritten: I love this emoji. I do not know why.]

MAN
Hahahah. Laughing with tears.
Do you like sushi? There's a delicious sushi place in my neighborhood.

FATHER
Sushi!

39

WOMAN

I love sushi.

FATHER

I love tuna sashimi.

WOMAN

Especially tuna sashimi.

FATHER

I haven't had tuna sashimi since I was demoted and sent to the mines after your outburst at school about why the motherland isn't doing anything to get the buses running again.

MAN

Sashimi is their specialty! So wanna go?

I'm told This sushi sequence was the most difficult to memorize

Thank you Actors.

FATHER

I say yes to sashimi.

NANHEE

You are not coming.

MAN

I dropped you a pin on maps.

FATHER

Yes I am.

MAN

Did you get it?

NANHEE

No you are not. This is a date! For Two people.

FATHER

So? I have already seen you in bed with this guy. Let me watch you eat sashimi!

MAN

What do you think?

WOMAN

Sorry. Something came up. Raincheck?

CHORUS

-First snow of the year!

CHORUS
-It is only October our earth is dying. WAKE UP / PEOPLE
-Minersdaughter, your one month free trial membership has expired. Would you like to renew your subscription?

WOMAN
Renew subscription

CHORUS
-Dear Miss Yoo, office is out of coffee and orange juice again, would you take care of that asap?

WOMAN
Reply to all

CHORUS
-*(Kakaotalk notification)* Katok! Katok!
-Hey Nanhee, it's Ji Ah. Have you heard from Mister Lee at all?

FATHER
He's a fraud.

NANHEE
What?

WOMAN
Dear team.

FATHER
Mister Lee. He's a fraud.

WOMAN
Thank you for your fraud.

NANHEE
Fuck.

WOMAN
Delete delete
Thank you for bringing this to my attention. I will restock asap.

CHORUS
-Heejin Cook has been tagged in Jimmy Kai's album.
-Jimmy Kai commented: Taco Tuesdays with the fabulous Cook Ladies. You have not lived till you've had Heejin's Kimchi Guacamole! Bulging hearts for eyes.

HEEJIN

Heejin Cook likes this.

MAN

You ...

MINSUNG

like this.

MAN

Poke Heejin Cook.

NANHEE

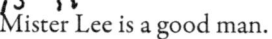

Mister Lee is a good man.
He was recommended by a fellow defector.

CHORUS
-*(Kakaotalk notification)* Katok! Katok!

CHORUS
-Hey Nanhee, it's Ji Ah. Don't know if you heard but Lee went AWOL. Some say he ran a scam, some say he got caught and gave info on all the families he delivered to. Everyone is freaking out. Let me know if you hear anything, k? yours, Ji Ah.

Gunshot.

FATHER

Uh oh.

NANHEE

Mister Lee is a good man.

MAN

Minersdaughter where did you go?

WOMAN

Minersdaughter is unavailable to chat.

CHORUS
-Miss Yoo, were you unable to find coffee and orange juice? Some colleagues are complaining

FATHER

Do you think Mister Lee betrayed you?

NANHEE

No.

MAN

I went on another Genie date. I was thinking about you all night. Hope you are well.

FATHER

I think Mister Lee betrayed you.

NANHEE

He did not look like that kind of man.

FATHER

You don't look like that kind of daughter but look how you betrayed me.

NANHEE

You would never say that. My father would never say that.

FATHER

Four years is a long time. People change.
You've changed.

MAN

Where did you go?

CHORUS

-Dear Miss Yoo surely it cannot be that hard to -

WOMAN

Delete

CHORUS

-*(sung)* **10/ 11 00101**

MAN

You there? Hello? / Monkey with hands over eyes.

CHORUS

-*(sung)* **010/01 01 0**
-Dear Miss Yoo please respond immediate / ly to

WOMAN

Delete

CHORUS
-*(sung)* **10/11 00101**
-What's on your
-*(sung)* **10111 001010 01100** ... [*continued in chaotic cacophony*]

FATHER
I wouldn't recognize you. You barely recognized me.

NANHEE
Shut up.

CHORUS
-What's on your mind what's on your mind?

FATHER
You don't know if that guy on the phone was actually me, do you?

NANHEE
I said shut up!

WOMAN
Shut down.

CHORUS
-Are you sure you want to shut down your computer now?

MAN
MinersDaughter, come back.

WOMAN
Shut down.

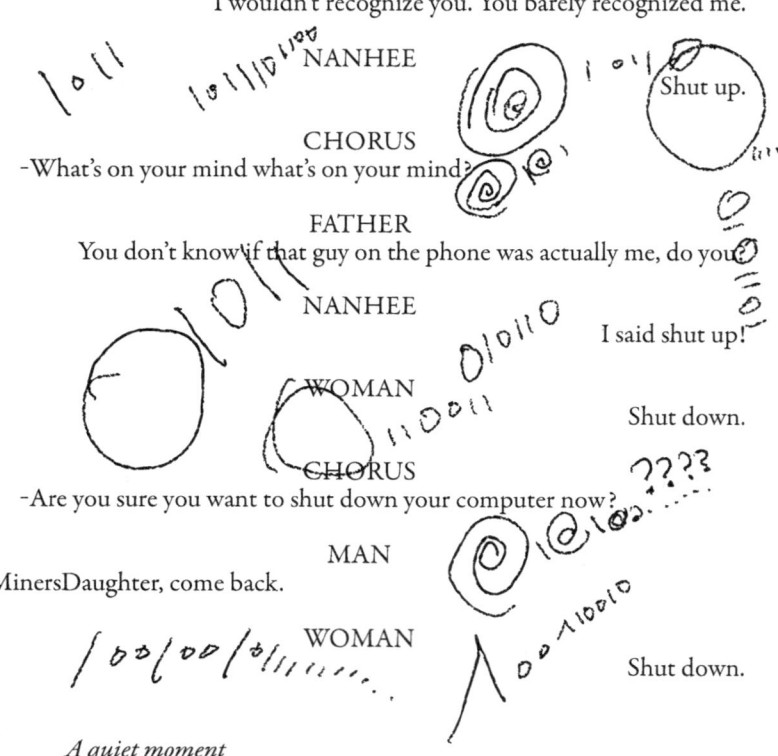

A quiet moment

soon interrupted by:

CHORUS
-Dear Miss Yoo. I am sorry to hear you have been feeling unwell. However, our office has zero tolerance for un-notified sick leave. Please be ready to attend evaluation committee with explanation about the past two days. Click here for format of apology letter.
PEEEEEEEEEEEP

NANHEE

MINSUNG

MINSUNG & NANHEE
I don't know how to say this

MINSUNG
      I am not a jealous man you know this

NANHEE
   but there are rumors concerning your honesty

MINSUNG
Heejin is my friend, on facebook I mean,
And there is all over her wall pictures of you and the-
Jimmy Kai,

NANHEE
        the other defectors
    They have had phone calls with their families
   But later on they turned out to be fake families

MINSUNG
he is a divorced man, I saw,
Because I went on his facebook, you are his friend on facebook
I did not even know you were on facebook

MINSUNG & NANHEE
And I need to know

NANHEE
     Did you find a fake father for me?

MINSUNG
   Do you just want to be my wife for my salary?

NANHEE
    You have not picked up the phone for several weeks
      And my fake father's number is not in service
And I have sent you so much money you fucking son of a dicksquash.

MINSUNG
Have I wasted my salary? Are you no longer my wife?

                    NANHEE
                                              I am sorry I cursed.

                    MINSUNG
I am sorry if I am overreacting

              MINSUNG & NANHEE
                Just please, tell the truth

                    MINSUNG
I feel old and useless. Please call me.

                    NANHEE
                                                    Please call.

                    CHORUS
    -Disconnected
    - *(Kakaotalk notification)* Katok! Katok! from Unknown.

                    CHORUS
-Miss Yoo, this is Lee. Do not attempt further contact. Your family's lives are at stake.

                    WOMAN
                                              Reply to Unknown:

                    NANHEE
                                              My family's lives?
                                              Why? What happened?

                    WOMAN
                                                         Send.

                    CHORUS
-Message cannot be sent.

                    WOMAN
                                                         Send.

                    CHORUS
-Message cannot be sent.

                    FATHER
                                                    Told you so.

Gunshot.

HEEJIN
Message from Heejin Cook WTF OMG dad untag me from that pic WTHIWWY?!?!??

MINSUNG
Hi!

HEEJIN
Delete! Plz! Idk wot u doin Imma unfriend u if u do shit lyk dis 2 me

MINSUNG
Huh?

HEEJIN
Picture! Photo! Photograph of me buttnaked with a banana in my face!

MINSUNG
Yes! You are three years old! I am happy you like it.

MAN
Smiley face with bulging hearts for eyes

HEEJIN
FML yr killin me. Sorry dad Im blockin u

MINSUNG
Heejin I don't understand what you are writing. Everything is okay?

CHORUS
-Sorry, this page isn't available
-The link you followed may be broken, or the page may have been removed.

MAN
Compose new email

MINSUNG
Dear daughter I don't know what happened but I can't find you any more. Daddy will fix and everything will be okay. I love you. From Dad

CHORUS
-Mail Delivery Subsystem MAILER DAEMON: the following address had permanent fatal errors

MINSUNG
Delete.

Gunshot.

NANHEE
Are you dead? Is that why you are here? Did they kill you?

FATHER
Didn't know you cared.

NANHEE
That's not fair.

FATHER
You left us to cross the river. You knew what that meant for us.

NANHEE
You said choose flying.
If I had to choose between family and flying, choose flying, you said.

FATHER
As in go to Pyongyang, have an awesome job, not sneak away into the river like a common traitor.

CHORUS
- *(sung) Jingle Bells Jingle Bells*
- Holiday special movie of the past, Watch Home Alone Two with your family / on channel
- 10 best end of year party venues in Seoul

MAN
Message from MrGooseMan, Merry Christmas.
Are you doing something special?

FATHER
Look, if you are happy in your paradise, that's one thing.

NANHEE
I am very happy.

FATHER
When you are not talking to fake fathers on the phone
you are talking to one in your head.
This is the happy that's worth the safety of your whole family?

NANHEE
What am I supposed to do? Go back?
I'm supposed to go back to North Korea?

Father kisses his daughter on her forehead, leaves.

CHORUS

Five Four Three Two One

Chorus celebrates new year with Auld Lang Syne.

MAN

Message from MrGooseMan, Happy New Year.
I watched the sunrise from Walnut Beach, Connecticut.
Did you watch the sunrise?
Message from MrGooseMan I cleaned my tiny room today!
It smells like floor wax. I love the smell of floor wax. Do you?
Message from MrGooseMan,

MINSUNG

I wrote a song. I think it's about you.

MAN

Smiley face.

MINSUNG

Well I know it's about you. I know it's about you because I wrote it for you.

MAN

Smiley face!

MINSUNG

It's not terrible. I used to make music before I made phones for Samsung.
I used to be in a band. I played the bass. That's how I stole my wife's heart.

MAN

Wink smiley face.
Recall previous message.
I used to have a band. I was the lead. I wrote lots of music.
That's how I got all the girls. Wink smiley face.

MINSUNG

But it's pretty stupid. I'm pretty stupid. I can't stop thinking about you.

MAN

Sad face.
Recall previous message.
I know it was a one night stand but I want more one night stands with you.

[Handwritten note: Sally Shen, Remember 2014? Lifted from Real Life Online interaction with an unrequited love who ghosted me.]

MINSUNG
Where did you go. Where did you go. Where did you go.
I wish you were more real for me.

CHORUS

(*Love Genie Jingle, sung*) *Ah~~*

WOMAN
MinersDaughter has logged in

[handwritten annotation: Goose prompt 2 — Locate a cringey interaction from your past and build it out into a comedic scene]

MAN & MINSUNG
Recall all unread messages!

WOMAN
Failed

MAN & MINSUNG
Recall all unread messages!

WOMAN
Failed

MAN & MINSUNG
Recall all unread

WOMAN
Recipient has read all messages.

MAN
Logout.

WOMAN
Message from MinersDaughter,
wow it's like you wrote a whole novel

MAN
MrGooseMan is no longer available to chat.

WOMAN
Message from MinersDaughter,

NANHEE
What's the song? Can I hear it?

[five]

MINSUNG

(singing)   *(translation)*

진짜라짜짜 진짜라니까 나	I am real
가짜라짜짜라니 맘이 아파와	You say I'm not real makes me sad
진짜 숨소리	Real breathing
진짜 마음이	Real feelings
진짜라짜짜보라니까 진짜야	Really real come see, I am real
왜 날 의심해	Why do you doubt me
왜 날 무시해	Why do you laugh at me
왜 날 잊으려해	Why try to forget me
하룻밤의 우리 소중한 추억	And our very precious one night
왜 날 싫어해	Why do you hate me
다 날 싫어해	Everyone hates me
내가 잘할게	I'll be better
하룻밤만 더 내게	One more night, give me
기회를 줘	One more chance
진짜라짜짜 진짜라니까 나	I am real
가짜라짜짜라니 눈물만 나와	You say I'm not real makes me cry
진짜 심장이	Real heart
진짜 나대니	Really beats
진짜라짜짜보라니까 진짜야	Really real come see, I am real

[six]

NANHEE
I like it.

MINSUNG
It's stupid.

NANHEE
Yes.

MINSUNG
Oh.

NANHEE
Stupid, in a funny way. It's a form of South Korean comedy. No?

MINSUNG
I wasn't intending the song for comedy.

NANHEE
Oh.

Minsung plays with his phone

CHORUS
-No new emails
-No new messages
-No new facebook notifications
-Sports Chosun Today: Something champion football golf blah blah

MINSUNG
What made you change your mind?

NANHEE
About what?

MINSUNG
You left the website, I left messages but you never checked them. Then you changed your mind.

NANHEE
Yes. I did.

MINSUNG

I was caught off guard. All those things I wrote, I was just writing, like poking on facebook
Do you do facebook? They have things called poking
It serves no purpose but to say hello I'm here.
I used to poke my daughter several times a day, before she blocked me.
Anyway.
So I was writing like I was poking, with no real purpose behind my words
So I was worried, when you said to meet up, even after you read my embarrassing poke-type messages, because most times when a girl wants to meet up after a very long time, It is because she has a baby.

NANHEE

I don't.

MINSUNG

Oh. Good.

She begins to take off his pants, he is taken by surprise.

MINSUNG

Woh!

NANHEE

Oh.

MINSUNG

What are you doing?!

NANHEE

This is not why you invited me here? That's why you wrote the song?

MINSUNG

I'm, sure, but

NANHEE

You don't want to?

MINSUNG

No no no of course I do,

NANHEE

I want to have sex.

MINSUNG

Yes.

NANHEE
Do you want to have sex?

MINSUNG
Yes.

NANHEE
Okay so.

She yanks his pants off

MINSUNG
Aahraaha!

NANHEE
What?

MINSUNG
You, my pants,

She looks at his penis.

NANHEE
It's not

MINSUNG
No!

NANHEE
That's okay. I will help.

She touches, fondles, tries,

NANHEE
Maybe should we turn off the lights?

Minsung claps.
Lights off.

NANHEE
That's cool.

MINSUNG
High efficiency.

NANHEE
May that be true of your penis.

CHORUS
Tick tock tick tock tock tick tock.

MINSUNG
Maybe if I, can I touch your, here?

NANHEE
Okay but you cannot steal this bra it's new.

MINSUNG
I didn't steal your -
Nevermind.

CHORUS
Tick tock tick tock tock tick tock.

NANHEE
You sure you don't have any medication to help the -

MINSUNG
No.

NANHEE
I wouldn't judge if you did.

MINSUNG
Great.

CHORUS
Tick tock tick tock tock tick / tock.

NANHEE
Wait, muscle spasm, let me switch sides

MINSUNG
No more please stop.

Clap.
Lights on.

NANHEE
How old are you again?

MINSUNG
It's got nothing to do with oldness, I'm fine like that in terms of oldness.

NANHEE
Are you not aroused by me?

MINSUNG
It's because you are coming on so fast.

NANHEE
Am I not attractive to you?

MINSUNG
I need to lead.

NANHEE
Do you think I am ugly?

MINSUNG
I will look that up for you, about sexual leaderships.

CHORUS
-search: /sexual leader

NANHEE
Is it because I did not have any plastic surgery?

MINSUNG
What?

NANHEE
Is it because I am North Korean? I am not sexual to you because I am North Korean?

MINSUNG
Of course / [not]

NANHEE
Why did you write all those things? Like a diary, you just wrote to some imaginary perfect woman but now that you see me you don't want any more? I am used goods for you now? Your one time North Korean taste? Am I one time usage, like the disposable contact lenses in the little plastic pods?

CHORUS
-Leadership in physical relationships will vary depending on

MINSUNG

You see here,

NANHEE

Even disposable contact lenses are used two or three times before it is discarded.

Nanhee takes his phone and chucks it into the toilet bowl.

MINSUNG

Hey!

NANHEE

Even disposable contact lenses! Do you think I'm less than disposable contact lenses?!

Nanhee cries.

MINSUNG

Oh.

He doesn't know what to do.
He finds a napkin, it's kind of used.
He hands it to her anyway.
He wants to rescue his phone but then decides it is inappropriate to rescue one's phone when one's lady is crying.
He pats her on the shoulder.

It's awkward.

MINSUNG (cont)

It is not because you are like disposable contact lenses.
I think you are very attractive.
I did not know you did not have any plastic surgery.
I wrote you a song. You don't write songs for people who you think are like disposable contact lenses.
It takes a lot of time and commitment to write a song.

Minsung desperately wants to play with his phone.

NANHEE

My father is gone.

MINSUNG

Oh! I'm so sorry.

NANHEE
No, gone from my mind. My mind is no longer broken. I want it to be broken again. I thought sex with you might break my mind again.

MINSUNG
That is very high expectation for second time.

NANHEE
I'm sorry. I'm sorry I threw your phone in the toilet.

MINSUNG
That's okay. It's, waterproof. Why do you want to break your mind?

NANHEE
I got used to having dinner with someone who knows me.

MINSUNG
Are you lonely?

NANHEE
Only recently. After my father appeared and then disappeared.

MINSUNG
How did you make him disappear?

NANHEE
I didn't. He said I was a traitor and I got angry and asked what do you want, do you want me to come back to North Korea? And as soon as I said that, he was gone. No goodbye, just gone. Now I am lonely.

MINSUNG
Fathers don't usually think their daughters are traitors.

NANHEE
The one in my head did.

MINSUNG
Maybe the one in your head wasn't your real father?

NANHEE
He still left an empty space, either way. And now I am the crazy lady who pulls down the pants of married men for the appearance of her father.

MINSUNG
I am sorry. Are you crying?

NANHEE
No. Maybe a little bit on the inside.

MINSUNG
What was it like back there?

NANHEE
North Korea?

MINSUNG
Your home.

NANHEE
Pretty big, for the village. A square house. Simple. We didn't have beds.

MINSUNG
No beds? We can do that.

Minsung folds the bed back into the wall,

MINSUNG
No beds. What else?

NANHEE
My mom would always give everyone hot water before sleep.

Minsung puts the kettle on.

MINSUNG
Okay.

NANHEE
And the nights were so dark.
We didn't have electricity so night would be so dark.

He claps. Dark.

MINSUNG
What else.

NANHEE
You could hear crows sometimes,

MINSUNG
Kakkaw Kakkaw

NANHEE
No more like, *[better crow sound]*

MINSUNG
Hey that's pretty good.

NANHEE
Thanks. And when everyone was asleep I would sneak out

MINSUNG
Sneak out!?

NANHEE
There was a boy.

MINSUNG
Ha!

NANHEE
North Korean teenagers know how to fall in love too.

MINSUNG
And you would sneak out to meet him.

NANHEE
In the dark.

MINSUNG
What did you talk about in the dark.

NANHEE
Dreams.

MINSUNG
About leaving?

NANHEE
No. You do not talk about such plans to anybody. Not family, not lovers. You never know who will report you. No we talked about real dreams. What we dreamt the night before.

MINSUNG
What kind of dreams.

NANHEE

I dreamt a lot about flying. One time I had a dream that my father gave me a pair of wings. He said Go! Fly! and I could not fly at all, and it turns out the wings were taken from a penguin. I said, what the fuck don't you know penguins cannot fly. Then he got upset, turned into a penguin and said I want my wings back and I said no! They're mine now! and ran away to Alaska. I guess that dream came true a little.

MINSUNG

You went to Alaska?

NANHEE

No. But it feels like that sometimes. Cold. Foreign.

MINSUNG

You know, fathers usually don't want their wings back. If my daughter had that dream I would want someone to tell her, hey dummy, fathers never ever want their wings back. Party it up in Alaska.

NANHEE

What about you? Tell me one of your dreams.

MINSUNG

I don't have dreams.

NANHEE

Make one up.

MINSUNG

My penis is awake and wants to make you happy.

NANHEE

Ha, that is your dream?

MINSUNG

No it is the truth. See?

NANHEE

Strange. It helped to tell you about my ex-boyfriend.

MINSUNG

Nothing like that. No, I think when you cried.
It is shameful but my penis is interested in devastated women.

NANHEE

I am not a –

MINSUNG
Let us not challenge the fragile penis.

NANHEE
Of course not.

a beautiful harmonious song, reminiscent of the Love Genie jingle.

MAN & WOMAN
(*sung*) *Ah ahah~ Ah ahah~*

oh wait. Minsung claps. Lights up.

NANHEE
Wha–?

He finds a condom

NANHEE
Oh.

MINSUNG
I am a responsible man.

NANHEE
Yes.

Clap, lights out.
Song continues, and then erupts into bliss.

MAN & WOMAN
(*sung*) *Ah ahah~ Ah ahah~ AH!*

MINSUNG
Wow.

NANHEE
That was nice.

MINSUNG
Yes. Do you think it worked?

NANHEE
I'm not sure.

MINSUNG
Shall we turn on the lights?

NANHEE
I'm nervous a little bit.

MINSUNG
Me too.

NANHEE
You too?

MINSUNG
Surprisingly so. It's the first time I've worked so hard at sex for the appearance of my lady's father.

Nanhee laughs.

MINSUNG
It feels great to be able to make someone laugh like that.

NANHEE
It feels great to be made to laugh like that.

MINSUNG
Your turn.

NANHEE
What is.

MINSUNG
To make me laugh like that.

NANHEE
Ok. Are you ticklish?

MINSUNG
Huh?

She tickles him.

MINSUNG
That's cheating! Ah stop! Stop stop!

Gunshot

Nanhee claps. Lights up.
There is a penguin head poking out of the toilet bowl. [hehehe]

PENGUIN HEAD

I want my wings back.

MINSUNG

Did it work? Is he here?

NANHEE

No, I think, there's a penguin. In your toilet.

Minsung hits the flush and the penguin is sucked into the toilet bowl. [hehehe 2]

NANHEE

Ho!

MINSUNG

Is it still there?

NANHEE

No. It's gone. I'm sorry. I'm probably just tired, seeing things,

MINSUNG

Do you want to sleepover?

NANHEE

Oh. Here?

MINSUNG

I mean it's a tight space, you don't have to but,
you live so far from here and if you're tired,
you are welcome to stay.
If you want.
Is what I'm saying?

NANHEE

I would love to.

[Out of anything I have ever written this scene is probably my most favorite.]

[seven]

Nanhee's dream.

North Korean military people with rifles march in singing the North Korean national anthem. Somewhere, her father appears, or is it a penguin?

CHORUS

(singing) — *(translation)*

아침은 빛나라 이 강산	Shine, Morning on this River and Mounts
은금에 자원도 가득한	Full of resources, Silver and Gold
삼천리 아름다운 내 조국	3000 miles of beauty is my motherland
반만년 오랜 력사에	A long history of Five Thousand years
찬란한 문화로 자라난	Glorious are the wise people
슬기론 인민의 이 영광	Bred in magnificent culture
몸과 맘 다 바쳐서	With all our body and heart
이 조선 길이 받드세	Let us serve our Chosun

PENGUIN

Nanhee!

Bang.

Penguin falls.

A Gun of Penguins

[eight]

Minsung and Nanhee at a comic book room.

MINSUNG
Tada!

NANHEE
It's, nice.

MINSUNG
You've seriously never been to a Comic Book room before.

NANHEE
I always thought comics were for children.

MINSUNG
What?! No!! It's life. It's love. It's fantasy and reality rolled up into one dusty florescent room full of shelves upon shelves of awesomeness. What?

NANHEE
Nothing. It's cute. You are being very cute.

MINSUNG
Oh. Sexy cute or emasculating cute?

NANHEE
Definitely sexy cute.

MINSUNG
That's what I thought.

CHORUS
Brinng Brinng
Brinng Brinng

MINSUNG
It's my wife.

CHORUS
Brinng Brinng
Brinng Brinng

NANHEE
Oh.

CHORUS
Brinng Brinng
Brinng

MINSUNG
She hung up.

NANHEE
Do you need to call her back?

MINSUNG
No.
Do you mind?

NANHEE
Go.

MINSUNG
Sorry. I'll be right back, just, um, browse?

A penguin appears.

NANHEE
He is not real.

They are now at Banpo Bridge.

NANHEE
Tada!

MINSUNG
It's nice.

NANHEE
You've seriously never been to Banpo Bridge before.

MINSUNG
Usually when I see the river I wish to jump in. And this bridge is notorious for such jumpers.

NANHEE
That is a morbid thought for such a beautiful view.

Bridge fountain show begins.

NANHEE
It begins!

MINSUNG
Oh wow that is so much water.

NANHEE
200 tons of river, 380 nozzles, and 190 light fixtures will dance in rhythm and tempo, to delight and amaze. The world's longest bridge fountain, welcome to Banpo's Moonlight Rainbow Fountain Show!
What?

MINSUNG
Nothing. You just, look very happy. It's a good look on you.

NANHEE
Ah yes. I perform happy very well. That's how I get people to fall in love with me.

MINSUNG
Oh. Am I falling in love with you?

NANHEE
I don't know why I said that. Falling in love, I pick up South Korean idioms like lint to sweaters -
Minsung kisses her.

NANHEE
Oh. Thank you. Good save.

MINSUNG
Are you accusing me of kissing to divert from talking about the problem of love?

CHORUS
- *(phone alert sound)*

NANHEE
Are you saying it wasn't a diversion?

CHORUS
-HeeheeHeejin has uploaded four new posts on Instagram

MAN
Open App

MINSUNG
Do you wish to talk about the problem of love?

CHORUS
- Image of Jimmy and your family in swimsuits.

NANHEE
I think, I do?

CHORUS
-HeeheeHeejin Commented "church volleyball competition. #slayed @JimKai"

MINSUNG
Woh.

NANHEE
But we don't have to talk about it if you don't want. It's okay.

MINSUNG
(distracted)
Okay.

MAN
Three More Images of Jimmy and your family in swimsuits.

Penguin appears.

CHORUS
-Someone draft this girl for the Olympics @HeeheeHeejin
-HeeheeHeejin commented: Thanks coach. @JimKai
-Unimportantperson007 commented: Holy Shit Heejin is that your dad? #hot #sorrynotsorry

MAN
Close app. Delete App.

PENGUIN
I'd rather fall into the river than fall in love with that guy. Hey. I'm talking to you. Hey. I want my wings back.

They are now at a Riverbank.

Minsung teaches Nanhee guitar.

MINSUNG
It's D minor, A minor and then. F. That's a little bit harder.

하룻밤의 우리 소.... **NANHEE & MINSUNG**
And our very precious...

MINSUNG
F.

Nanhee attempts F code badly.

NANHEE
소.... *precio...*

MINSUNG
F.

Nanhee attempts F code badly.

NANHEE
소.... *precio...*

MINSUNG
It's the

NANHEE
F! I know!

Nanhee attempts F code badly. and again and again and again

MINSUNG
Break?

NANHEE
No! I am not the giving up kind.

MINSUNG
I am worried I will lose my guitar to the water.

NANHEE
Why?

MINSUNG
You know, my phone, from before. I mean, it was a joke. It's okay.

NANHEE
Okay.

[handwritten notes: This is a very syntax even for translated Korean. Where did it come from? Why did I write this and make so many brilliant actresses say this nonsense? I do know but I love this line.]

MINSUNG
What better place to learn songs than by the river? Where you can throw things in when frustrated?

NANHEE
Is that still a joke?

MINSUNG
Yes.

NANHEE
Why do you keep making the same joke when I find it unfunny?

CHORUS
Brinng Brinng Brinng

MINSUNG
It's my wife.

NANHEE
What does your wife have to do with your unfunny jokes?

MINSUNG
Nothing. The phone call is from my wife. Nothing to do with my joke you didn't get.

PENGUIN
Wow. That's kinda mean.

NANHEE
Here we go.

MINSUNG
What do you mean by that?

NANHEE
What do you mean what do I mean?

MINSUNG
Are you trying to pick a fight?

NANHEE
No?

MINSUNG
Then what did you mean about here we go, because it is not my fault that sometimes she calls, we have a child we have to care for together,

MINSUNG (cont)
that means now, I can't apologize every time she calls, or every time you don't get my joke, none of those things are my fault?

NANHEE

So don't?

PENGUIN

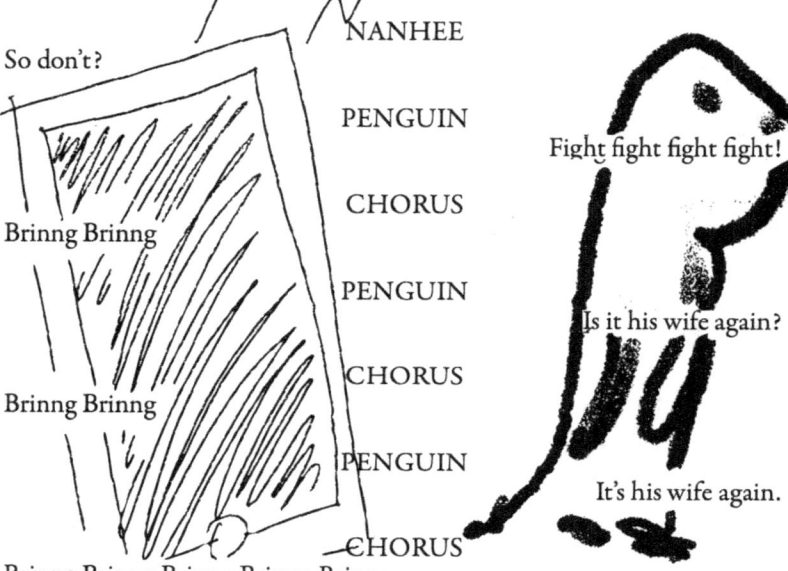

Fight fight fight fight!

CHORUS

PENGUIN

Brinng Brinng

Is it his wife again?

CHORUS

Brinng Brinng

PENGUIN

It's his wife again.

CHORUS
Brinng Brinng Brinng Brinng Brinng

Nanhee takes his phone and turns it off.

CHORUS
(phone turning off) Doorooroorooroooo.

MINSUNG

I'll go umm, get some beers.

He goes.

NANHEE

Go away.

PENGUIN
I will when I get my wings back.

CHORUS
-The account you're trying to reach is currently unavailable Leave a message after the
Peeeeeeeeeeeeeeeep

WIFE

I wish you would change your greeting.
Your voice is much nicer than the machine woman.
I am in Hartford. At the airport. Long term parking lot.
Is it worth saying,
When I called, I thought, this is a phone call telling you to pick me up at the Incheon airport. But then the machine lady said you were unavailable.
And now, I don't know what to do Minsung.
People should talk to people.
Every day that I wake up alone on my little bed I think, people should talk to people. And here we are talking to machine people
Who repeat the same greeting every time you are unavailable
and we say it is for our child
it is for our child that you are unavailable, that I am unavailable
a spell I have cast on my brain,
every phone call missed, every flight cancelled,
every motion a married couple ought to not engage themselves in
has been okayed by the spell
and has made me small.
Made you small.
I don't want to be small any more.
I don't want to make you small any more.
Heejin and I are moving to Texas.
With Jimmy.
I'm sorry.

[handwritten: This monologue was originally a page and a half long. Every workshop, it got shorter and shorter until it became this. I mourn this monologue]

CHORUS

peep peep peep peep peeeeep peeeeeeeeeeeeep
peeeeeeeeeeeeeeeeeeeeeeeeeeeep
peeeeeeeeeeeeeeeeeeeeeeeeeeeeeeeeeeeeeeeeeeeeeeeeee/eeeeep

NANHEE

... but that's not the real ending of the story.

MINSUNG

Hm?

Minsung and Nanhee are in a bed.

[handwritten: This page is dedicated to the words I loved that I let go. (Goodbye)]

NANHEE

In the original story, the angel goes back. Once a year. But my father, he left that part out. Why? Why do that?

MINSUNG

Sorry what I wasn't listening.

NANHEE
Why?

MINSUNG
Because it's three am.

NANHEE
Why would he change the ending? He didn't want us to return, right? If we made it to paradise, he wanted us to stay. He would never want his wings back.

MINSUNG
What?

NANHEE
The penguin that I told you about wants his wings back but obviously it's not my real father and the original ending is stupid because why would anyone do that? Because Duh, who leaves paradise, just to see their family?

MINSUNG
People who miss their family?

NANHEE
Ha! I very nearly killed myself crossing three borders to get here
Spent a whole year of my life tricking my tongue to speak differently
Spent another three years, tricking my brain to think differently
And now I work for the government.
Do you know how many defectors work for the government?
Do you have any idea how amazing it is that I made it to the place where I can serve orange juice and coffee to the cubicle workers of the South Korean Government?
Look at this face.
This is the face of the hero who has climbed over impossible walls to find success in paradise. It is not the face of the idiot who risks paradise because she misses her family, no?

MINSUNG
I love you.

NANHEE
What? I was saying something. I was trying to tell you something.

MINSUNG
Isn't this more important? That I love you? That I finally was brave enough to say I love you?

NANHEE
Why is that brave?

MINSUNG
Because. It is.

NANHEE
you love me.

MINSUNG
Yes.

NANHEE
Ok.

MINSUNG
Do you love me?

NANHEE
No.

MINSUNG
Oh.

NANHEE
I don't know you. You don't know me.

MINSUNG
Love isn't about knowing someone it's

NANHEE
It's what then. What is it about.

MINSUNG
It's just, feelings, I have feelings, about you and I'm telling you

NANHEE
Feelings. Okay. You have feelings. What does that do?

MINSUNG
What do you mean, what does it

NANHEE
If I have feelings with you too what does that do? Does it make my life better somehow, my life that is as meaningful as the tip of a toenail that is clipped off during a pedicure?

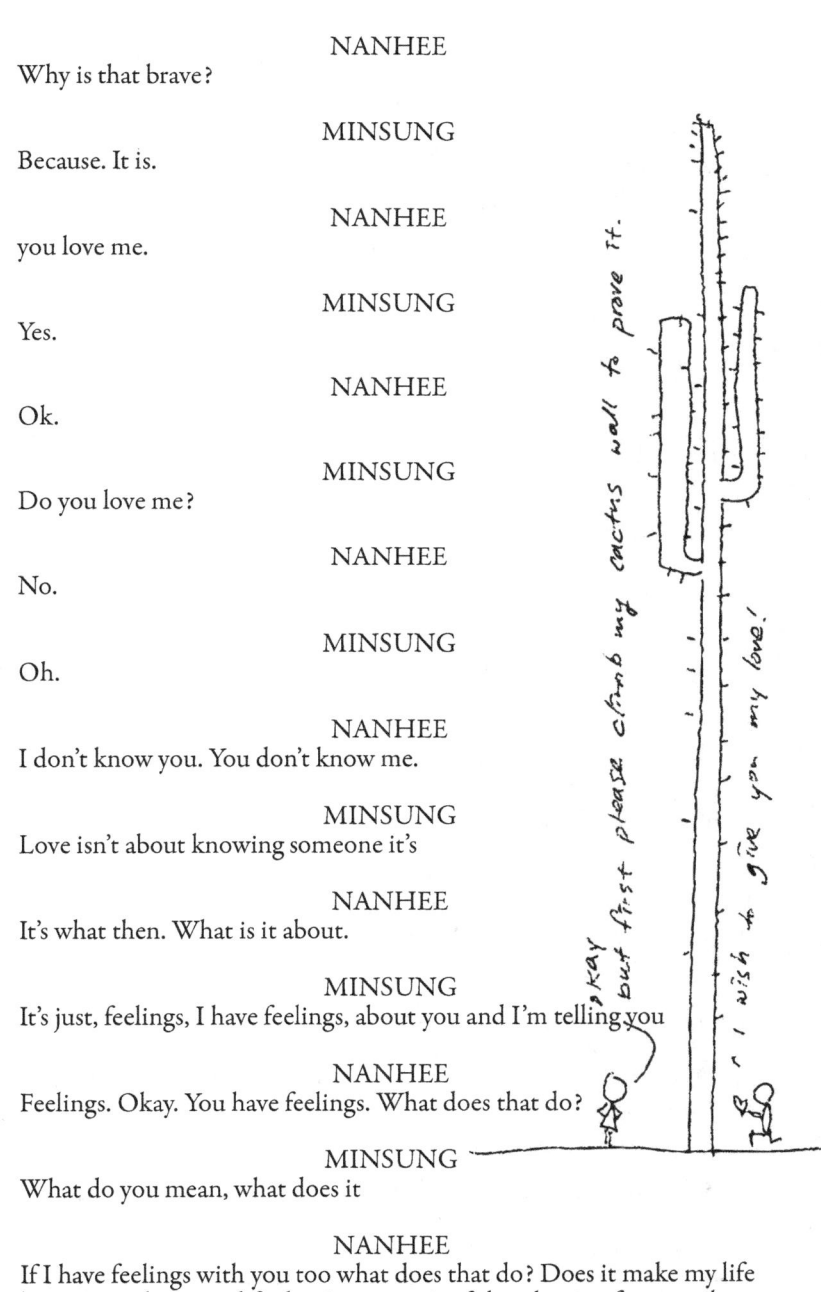

MINSUNG
Why are you so upset?

NANHEE
We are not together because of love. We are together because we are alone and being together paralyzes that terrible feeling for a while.

MINSUNG
You know what forget it.

NANHEE
You want this temporary paralysis to be love

MINSUNG
I said / forget

NANHEE
You hope that by saying this, "I love you," something is going to change, but nothing will change, the flame will die and that is just hope torture isn't it?

MINSUNG
How are you so sure it will die?

NANHEE
You're married. I am freezing to the color blue and you are running around shouting "Look Look We found one matchstick!!" but look around, where is the wood where is the coal,

MINSUNG
What does that even mean? I just confessed my love. Who reacts like this to a confession of love? What is wrong with you?

NANHEE
Nothing is wrong with me! South Koreans are obsessed with love. I love. You love. All because of love. But then you find love, then you send them away to another country, and live alone in a closet with a shower hanging over it, / that is not real love

MINSUNG
Right because North Koreans so great at Real Love. You can't even tell your boyfriend, or in fact, your own father that you are escaping the country because he might report you and you are probably never going to see him or anyone you ever "loved" ever again, and you can't give two shits about what you did to people you left, what are you doing?

NANHEE

Leaving.

MINSUNG

This is your house.

NANHEE

Keep it.

MINSUNG

What? Don't be crazy

NANHEE

Do not call me crazy.

MINSUNG

I'm getting a divorce.

NANHEE

?

MINSUNG

My wife.
She is divorcing me.
She has found a better man who can –
I'm sorry about-.
Sorry.
Stay.

NANHEE

When?

MINSUNG

Last week. She told me last week.

NANHEE

Are you okay?

MINSUNG

No.

NANHEE

Are you crying?

[handwritten note: I think this scene works best when Minsung really loves Nanhee and Nanhee really really wants to believe it.]

[handwritten: STAY...]

MINSUNG

No.
Maybe a little bit on the inside.

CHORUS

-No new emails
-No new messages

MINSUNG

I feel old and useless.

CHORUS

-No new facebook notifications. Refresh browser

NANHEE

Is that why? Why you said you love me?

MINSUNG

Do you really feel like your life is as meaningful as the tip of a toenail that is clipped off during a pedicure?

NANHEE

No. Sometimes.

MINSUNG

It is not true. You have impact. You make me feel less old and less useless. Do I have impact on you?

NANHEE

Yes.

MINSUNG

Couldn't we call that love, for now, and see what happens? Couldn't that be enough, for now?

NANHEE

-

MINSUNG

Okay. I take it back. I will feel the feelings only inside, and I cancel saying I love you. But when I find wood and or coal I will say it again.

NANHEE

You know that it is not actual wood and or coal, it was a metaph-

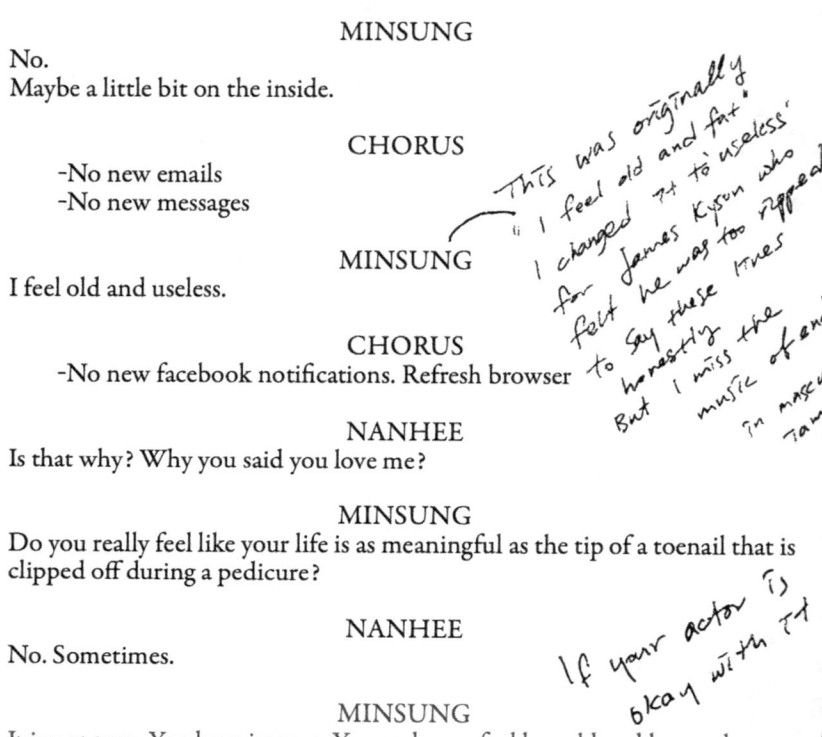

This was originally "I feel old and fat." I changed it to "useless" for James Kyson who felt he was too ripped to say these lines honestly. But I miss the music of an "m" sound. I am

If your actor is okay with it

Try my original :)

MINSUNG

Yes. Thank you. I know.

NANHEE

I just had this image of you stacking up coal in your collapsible bed and confessing more love

MINSUNG

I won't. I promise.

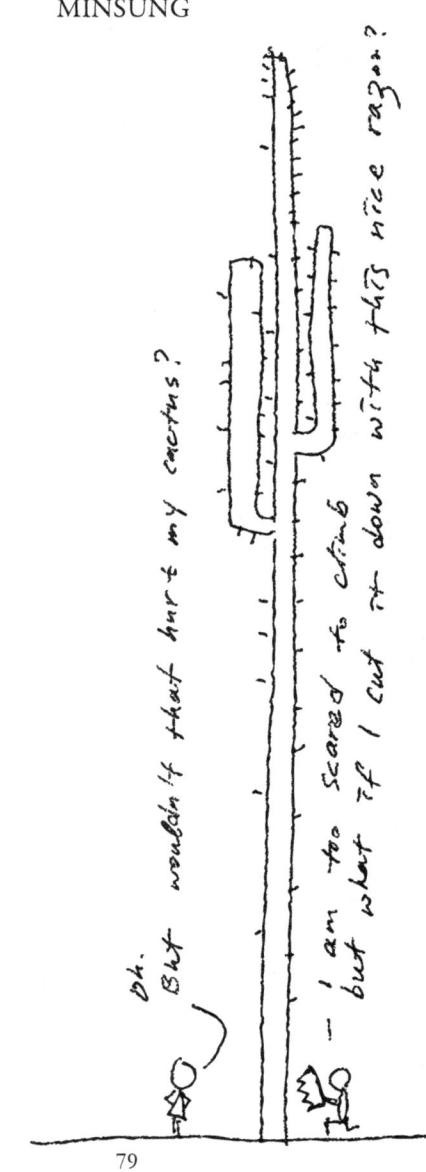

[nine]

Nanhee's dream

                              CHORUS (penguins)
(singing)   *(translation)*
진짜라짜짜짜 진짜라니까 나   **I am real**

                                FATHER

I was born in Pyongyang,
I have a wife, and six children. Four boys, two girls.
I was a flute player in the military band in Pyongyang,
but we relocated after an incident at my daughter's school where she asked a question about why the fatherland isn't doing anything to get the buses running again.

His head is dunked into a toilet bowl

                                CHORUS
(singing)   *(translation)*
가짜라짜짜라니   **You say I'm not real**

head resurfaces

                                FATHER
And we loved our relocation very much but then the daughter disappeared one day I don't know where she is.

                                CHORUS
(singing)   *(translation)*
맘이 아파와   **makes me sad**

                                FATHER
She was kidnapped. I am sure of it. She was ensnared in the clutches of a secret agent of the puppet government and dragged to South Korea. I am sure of it. I don't know where she is.

His head is dunked into a toilet bowl

                                CHORUS
(singing)   *(translation)*
진짜라짜짜짜짜 보라니까 진짜야   **I am real look I am real**

And then resurfaces
He is a penguin head.

FATHER

Every day in South Korea is a nightmare. It is a society of darkness, not only to the people like my daughter who has been dragged there, but to the South Korean people themselves.

Gunshot
Father's Penguin head is blown off

FATHER (cont)

To evil daughter who is subject to this humiliation, I implore you, come back to the Fatherland.
Come back to the Fatherland
Come back to the Father.
I want my wings back.

Nanhee wakes up.

A gift doodle from the remarkable Francis Jue who had his head dunked in toilet bowl 8 times a week because of these words I wrote in italics... Remarkable!

Nanhee goes back to her Fatherland.

Hi Hansol!
Do you remember the many many monologues that used to live here?
I loved them all and they live on in my mind like Minsung does in Nanhee's.
Paul Cosker xoxo

[ten]

Minsung on Youtube

MINSUNG

Hello everyone.
My name is Guk Minsung.
I am a goose father.
My wife took our daughter and left me for a Japanese-American in Texas.
I have a lady.
She left me too.
She went back to North Korea to bring back her family and said that I should write a song for her if I get sad because that is what I did before and it helped. It has been a month, since she left me a note on her side of my bed and disappeared. So I wrote a song, in hopes it might help. I don't think it will because I don't think they have YouTube in North Korea and writing songs only works when you believe that the person you wrote it for can hear it, but.

It's not terrible. The song. I used to be in a band so.
(hello to my buddies from Pigskin Barbeque if you're seeing this)
Anyways. Here's my song.

MINSUNG

(singing)	*(translation)*
나나나 죽고 싶다이아이야	I I I wanna die
나나나 죽고 싶다이아이야	I I I wanna die
나나나 죽고 싶다이아이야	I I I wanna die
나나나 죽고 싶다	I I I wanna die

CHORUS

-Park Jiyun likes this
-Um Joosong likes this

MINSUNG

죽을만큼 그립지는 않아	Not dying to see you
죽을만큼 걱정되지 않아	Not dying of worry
죽을만큼 슬프지도 않은데	Not dying of sadness
나나나죽고 싶다이아이야	But I I I wanna die

CHORUS

-Kim Hanee / likes this
-Kate Lim likes this

MINSUNG

나나나 죽고 싶다	I I I wanna die

CHORUS

-Jin / likes this
-June / likes this
-John Park / likes this
-26 shares

MINSUNG

죽었는지 궁금하긴 해 가끔 — Wonder if you're dead sometimes

CHORUS

-1067 views

MINSUNG

죽었으면 꿈에 나타나 — If you are, come to my dreams

CHORUS

-Fritz / likes this
-Kai / likes this
-Zahir / likes this

MINSUNG

죽었다고 말해주라 나 지금 — Tell me you are dead coz

CHORUS

-5300 / views
-181 shares

MINSUNG

나나나 죽고 싶다이아이야 — I I I wanna die

CHORUS

-Ping likes this
-Kobe likes this

MINSUNG

나나나 — I I I

CHORUS

(sung) ***Like Share Click***

MINSUNG

죽고 싶다 — wanna die

CHORUS

- Call mama if you get lonely sweetie
- Dude's face at 1'56 is my screensaver LoL

CHORUS
- This isn't real. North Korea is a closed country, god people are idiots.
- TBH mad addicted to this song

Like Share Click share this don't die Like Share Click share this don't die
Like Share Click share this don't die Like Share Click share this don't die

- This is so sad I was adopted from Korea so I know
- Don't die!
- I'll totally sleep with you
- Is this real?
- So sad. He's kinda funny though.

Like Share Click share this don't die
Like Share Click tag this don't die share this don't die
Like Share Click tag this share this don't die don't die

- So real. Check him out on Good Morning Seoul. Click here to go to link.
- I totes wanna learn that dance for prom
- Someone put him out of his misery ugh

Like Share Click dig it don't die share this don't die
Like Share Click share this don't die
Like Share Click dig it don't die share this don't die
Like Share Click share this don't die Like Share Click don't die

MINSUNG
63빌딩에서 날아볼까   Should I fly from 63 Building

CHORUS
-Wife's a fucking cunt poor guy

MINSUNG
반포대교로 갈까   Take a trip to Banpo Bridge

CHORUS
-What you get for fucking a commie
-54 people like this

MINSUNG
사회 물의 끼치지 말고   Or don't be a social nuisance
청산가리 한두 사발 마실까 하 하   chug a bowl of acid instead haha

CHORUS
-Jesus loves you stay strong
-In bed

육이오가 지난지가 언젠데	**MINSUNG** Been so long since the war	

CHORUS
-North Korean girls are Hot
-Click here for hot Asian porn

우리 여태 이 모양인가	**MINSUNG** How are we still stuck here	

CHORUS
-I love Kpop. Please upload more vids!

나도 나도 나도 나도	**MINSUNG** Should I I I I I I I also	

북한이나 갈까 북한이 나을까	**MINSUNG** Should I go North too? Would that be better?	

CHORUS
-I went to NK last year. Place is fucked up. Like Hunger Games fucked up.
-I find this video hilarious is that terrible? No yes yes 1011

CHORUS	MINSUNG	CHORUS
- Kara / likes this		
- J.D / likes this		0110
- Malachi / likes this	북한으로 가면 니가 있나	01001101
- 1089 shares	If I go North will you be there?	
		01100100
Like Like share 101	북한남과 눈맞았을까	11010110
don't die	Have you found a Northern Man?	01001101
		01100100
Yuri Liam 011 Likes	죽다 살아 나서 여기 왔는데	
this 1 die	Survived so many deaths to be here	
		11010110
1011 tag 0 die	왜 다시 죽으러 갔냐 이 가시나	01001101
	so why you go to die, stupid girl	
0 it like 0 click 10110	야야야 죽고 싶냐이아이야	01001 01001
	hey hey hey Do you wanna die	
		01001
		010010100

CHORUS

100,000 + views!

MINSUNG

죽을만큼 그립지는 않아	Not dying to see you but
그치만 그리우니까	But I do miss you, so
죽지 않았으면	If you did not die
집에 와.	Come home.

MINSUNG (cont)

That's the song.
I hope you liked it.
I hope you liked my song Nanhee, if you can see this.
I miss you, and I'm sorry I wasn't enough.

He takes a gun to his temple.
Shoots.
A cute stream of water shoots into his face.

MINSUNG (cont)

Oh. I thought that would have more impact.

He shoots couple more times into the air.

MINSUNG

It's a water gun.
Just a little, performance art.

Um. Okay.
Pigskin Barbeque forever. Rah.

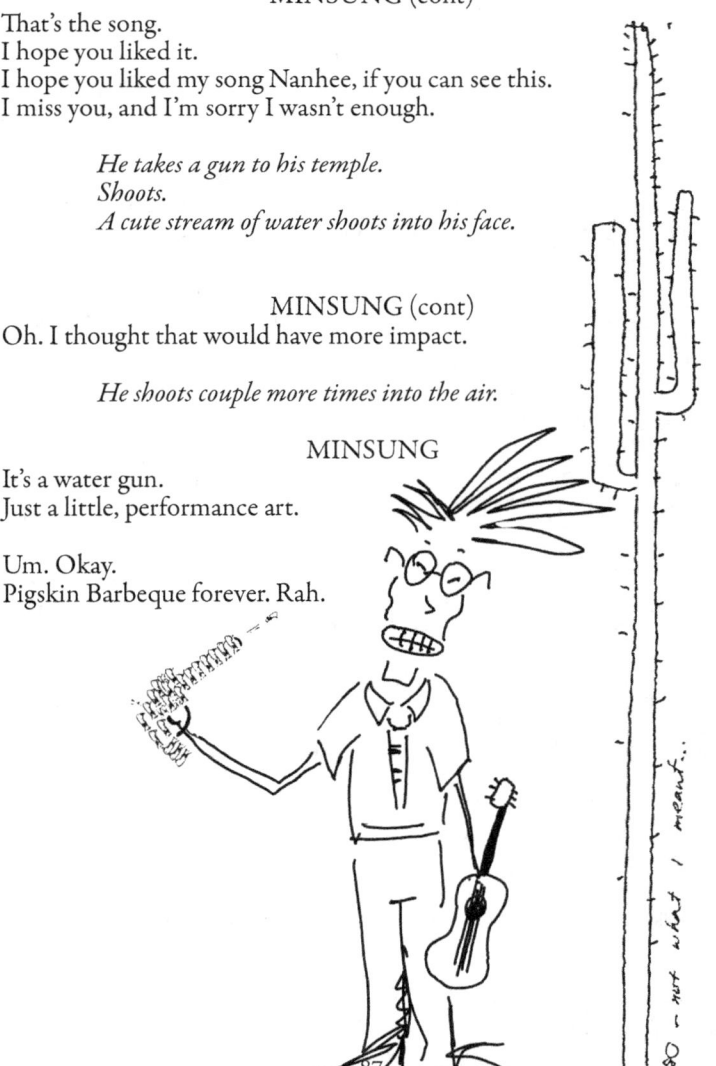

[eleven]

CHORUS
-Goose guy "suicide song" viral among teenagers and Hongdae dance venues.
-Students raise awareness for North Korean defectors at Yonsei University
-Goose Guy signs contract with Melon.com for single of "I wanna Die"
-Defector speaks out against Mr Goose Guy's ignorance in his response rap, "So Die"

NANHEE

Dear MrGooseMan
I am home.
I found my father in the kitchen, making seaweed soup for his birthday
He was so surprised to see me.
And so surprised to see all the money I brought!
He is keeping it safe until we figure out a plan to leave here for good.
For now, I am hiding in my childhood room.
It is smaller than I remember, this room.
It is not smaller than your *koshiwon*.
I wish I could send this letter to your *koshiwon*
Sadly I can't because I am in North Korea and your *koshiwon* is not.
But maybe if I think my letters loud enough you will hear them.
I am sorry I left without saying goodbye.
But I will see you again so soon!
Don't feel old and useless.
From Miner's Daugher.

p.s. there was never a phone.
Mister Lee was, as suspected, a son of a dicksquash and I wish him to hell but I am glad my dreams were not real.

CHORUS
-First snow of the year!
-It is only October our earth is dying. WAKE UP / PEOPLE

MAN
Minsung, what's on your mind?

CHORUS
-Sunday Night Docu: Who was Yoo Nanhee? Lover or Spy?

MAN
Where are you mister GooseMan? Thousands of elite women are waiting for your poke of love.

CHORUS
-It's my first Celebrity sighting! Goose guy buying beers at seven eleven near Banpo Bridge.
-Attached: picture of goose guy in pjs and sad hair
-Retweet
-Retweet
-Retweet

MAN
Minsung, you have 747 new friend requests
Are you sure you would like to de-activate your account?

MINSUNG
Yes.

MAN
Are you sure?

MINSUNG
Yes I'm sure.

MAN
But what if she tries to pm you through facebook?
What if she tries to find you and you are a broken page for her?

MINSUNG
Cancel account de-activation.

NANHEE
Dear GooseMan
He doesn't want us to cross over.
He wants to use the money for practical things, like food and clothing, not certain death in the winter river.
Meanwhile, I am still imprisoned in my childhood room.
It's been a few months since I heard your voice.
Do you remember my voice?
Have you found a new friend to send emojis to?
If not, don't.
From miner's daughter

CHORUS
- *(sung) **Jingle Bells Jingle Bells***
-Holiday special movie of the past, Watch Home Alone Two with your family on channel

MAN

Minsung! What are you doing for Christmas?

CHORUS

-Do things!
-Buy things!
-Look at all these other people who are happier than you!

MAN

Are you sure you want to log out of facebook instead of stalking pictures of your family's new family on their first Christmas without you?

CHORUS

-Gooseguy's daughter is a serious hottie. #Whosthedaddy?
#4realztho
 link to pic
-Retweet
-Retweet
-Retweet
Five Four Three Two One

MAN

Minsung! What are you doing for New Year's?

CHORUS

-Do things!
-Buy things!
-Look at more other people who are happier than you!
bring bring bring bring bring bring bring

MINSUNG

Passport, die. Passport no good for going America.
They think my friend was an intelligence hazard, **Spy**,
For North Korea. Spy.
no no **Spy No. Daddy Friend No Spy**
but they just want me to be nearby when they have questions.
I would be on a plane right now if I could. I love Texas. I love you.
Could you come here for a week or so?
Whenever you want.
No no don't give the phone to your mother I can -
Hi.
I just thought, For a week or so.
I am sorry I am such an embarrassment.

Will you
Will you just, put my daughter back on the phone.
Will you put our daughter back on the

90

CHORUS
-Disconnected

NANHEE
The penguins are gone, and the father is real,
And I thought that was all I ever wanted
It turns out, not.

CHORUS
tick tock tick tock tock tick tock tick

NANHEE
Hey, remember when I came to your *Koshiwon* and demanded sex for the appearance of my father?
I wish there was a way to demand the appearance of you, right now.

CHORUS
Tick Tock Tick Tock Tock Tick Tock Tick

NANHEE
Should I just swim across the river without a broker or my father?
I don't know if I have it in me to swim across any more rivers Minsung.
I feel old and useless.

Hellloooooo. Can you hear me?

MAN
Minsung, you have

CHORUS
-no new emails
-no new messages
-no new facebook notifications

NANHEE
I am thinking a thousand letters to you like your poke type messages

CHORUS
-Students raise awareness for something else at Yonsei University

NANHEE
But I feel crowded with my own voice and cannot remember yours

CHORUS
-Someone else's something else viral among teenagers and
 Hongdae dance venues

MAN
Guess our fifteen minutes are up, huh?

NANHEE
I cannot even remember some parts of your face

CHORUS
-Heejin Cook is not available to chat

NANHEE
I miss your *koshiwon*, the smell of floor wax
Your voice,
I miss, you.

MAN
What's on your mind?

NANHEE
Love, Nanhee

MAN
Minsung, what's on your-

Gunshot.

CHORUS
-One hit wonder Guk Minsung found with a gunshot wound in his Shinchun *koshiwon*
-Alleged suicide of Guk
-Alleged assassination of Guk
-Goose fathers, how bad is it really?

NANHEE
Dear Minsung,
I saw your YouTube song about wanting to die.
(please don't die)
My father found it in the black market.
He asked me if I was your lady.
I said, yes. I also said you are getting a divorce.
He shook his head but I could see him smile a little
as he opened a jar of alcohol
and when we were both dizzy with warmth
I finally told him about my dreams with the penguins
and he laughed and laughed
and he said
fathers never want their wings back.

                    NANHEE (cont)
         and then he lifted the floorboard he was sitting on
and gave me the exact amount of money that I gave him when I first
                                                         arrived.
                             he did not spend any of it.
                                                    And he said
                                                            go,
                                                            fly.

                                      I will see you so soon.
                                            Your Nanhee.

                          CHORUS
-Nation mourns the death of beloved Goose Guy with a candlelight
vigil
-Guk Minsung; a life
-Guk Minsung; a death
-Guk Minsung's life to be made into a blockbuster starring Song
Kangho

                          MINSUNG
Hi, this is Guk Minsung. Thanks for calling but I can't come to the
phone right now. Leave a message after the

                          CHORUS

PEEP

                          HEEJIN
Hi dad.
I just called to say hi.
I never did that, I think. Call to say hi.
Okay bye.

                          MINSUNG
Hi this is Guk Minsung Thanks for calling but I can't come to the phone
right now. Leave a message after the

                          CHORUS

PEEP

                          HEEJIN
Hi dad.
Just came back from your funeral.
They didn't let mom in but they let me in so I put a flower by your photo.
I wrote my name on the stem so you would know which was mine.
I wrote it in Korean. Guk. Hee. Jin. Looks like a five year old wrote it
but,
Um.
Okay bye.

MINSUNG

Hi this is Guk Minsung Thanks for calling but I can't come to the phone right now. Leave a message after the

CHORUS

PEEP

HEEJIN

I got into UT. It's short for University of Texas.
It's a pretty big deal. Mom and Jimmy bought me a car. Prius.
Um. Your phone gets disconnected tomorrow.
I'm glad I got to tell you I got in.
Um.
Okay. Bye.
Um.
Actually. I also want to say, because I don't know where else to say,
Um
I'm really angry, I think.
I can't forgive you for this.
I didn't really know you. I know I was a bitch to you. So I am sorry.
But now I have to be sorry forever.
I don't know how to-
Um.
Okay bye.

CHORUS

-The number you are trying to reach is no longer in service.
 Please try again.

NANHEE

I'm back.
Like I said I'd be.
It took a long time.
Like I said it might.
I just wanted to say that I think what you did was very stupid.
I saw your YouTube video.
You look very handsome.
I like your song.
I am sorry it didn't help.

CHORUS

-The number you are trying to reach is no longer in service.
 Please try again.

[twelve]

Nanhee at Banpo Bridge, alone in the crowds.
Next to her is the Penguin, dressed up in a very penguin-like tuxedo.
They look at the bridge fountain.

PENGUIN
Are we waiting for the fountain?

NANHEE
No. It's winter. They shut it down for the winter.

PENGUIN
Then what are we doing here? Are we waiting for spring?
Are we waiting for you to stop feeling like a tip of a toenail that is clipped off during a pedicure?
Are we waiting for him?

NANHEE
He's dead.

PENGUIN
Your mind can re-create fathers, penguins, father-penguin hybrids in varied states of terrifying.

NANHEE
I don't mind this version too much.

PENGUIN
Thank you. Me too. Don't evade. I'm just saying, you could probably re-create other things if you wanted.

Nanhee's mind makes the bridge fountain begin!

PENGUIN
Oh nice. But I meant the other, other thing.

MINSUNG
Leave her alone. Maybe she's not ready to see the other, other thing.

NANHEE
Oh.

PENGUIN
Yay you did it!

MINSUNG
Your penguin's back.

PENGUIN
I was just leaving. *(to Nanhee)* I'll be right here if you need me sweetie. *(to Minsung)* You. Don't fuck it up.

Penguin gives them some space.

MINSUNG
(re: penguin) You really need some new friends.

NANHEE
Why did you – [do it?]

MINSUNG
Oh you know, I was lonely.
Did you find him? Your real dad?

NANHEE
Yes.

MINSUNG
Was it nice to see him?

NANHEE
Yes.

MINSUNG
Did he want his wings back?

NANHEE
No.
If nothing else I have helped you understand metaphor.
My life has had impact. It is not completely meaningless.

MINSUNG
Thank you for your impact.

NANHEE
Thank you for yours.
I'm sorry we didn't get to call it what you wanted to call it.

MINSUNG
Maybe it's not too late. Do you still have it?

Nanhee pulls out a match.

NANHEE

Oh. It's so nice.

MINSUNG

Very. Are you thinking you could take our very nice very pretty match to light it with some new guy?

This makes her laugh.

MINSUNG

Coz I'm okay with that. I can be okay with that. Eventually.

NANHEE

Thank you. But this one is for you.

She lights the match.
He claps.
All the lights go dark, except the flame from the match.

NANHEE

I will miss you. For a really long time.

MINSUNG

Thank you.

He kisses her on the head

NANHEE

Go. Fly.

Minsung leaves the light.

Alone, Nanhee lets the glow of the flame fill her up with hope. then gently, she blows out the match, like a kiss to his heart.

Good Bye.

_____ *End of play*

Kindly rotate your book to the RIGHT.

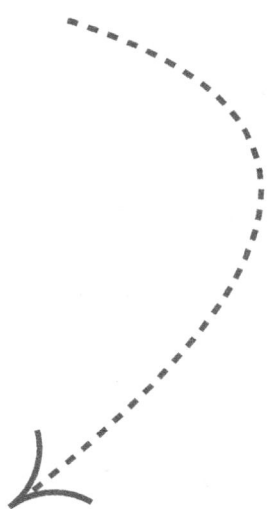

(I think it was one of the original doodles for our set at Soho Rep...)

A soft doodle from the beautifully obsessive brain of Dustin 1/7/15

CHARACTERS

ASH   Non-Binary, 20s. Southpaw Boxer.
ROBIN   Female, 30s. Ash's older wife.
RYAN   Male, Early to mid 30s. Robin's younger brother.
PETER   Male, Late 30s. A father.
WOLF   a mix of the familiar with the terribly unexpected

* Cast should be racially diverse.
* Wolf should be of East Asian descent

[Where We Are]

hello wolf.

WOLF

What if I said I am not what you think you see.
I am not an actor human, this floor is forest earth, and
to the left of that glaring exit light, a river flows, the width and length and velocity of the Egyptian NILE

You are not what you feel you are, you are a spider the size of your eyelash. Or an eagle flying two thousand feet above our heads. Or the mother of the newest freshest pinecone dangling over that aisle. We are riding on the back of a giant turtle, hurtling through the cosmos, in a **four point five four billion year race** against the tiniest of the tiniest white easter rabbits.

What if I said,

    you are the single most important breath in my space.
    you are the first gear that turns the clock of my world.
    you are the final drop of dew that breaks down the universal dam of miscommunication.
    I need you with every blood cell and cranial nerve I possess.

And you believed me?

Does that change anything?

WOLF (cont)

What if I said Oops, actually no, we are sitting in a rented space on top of concrete ground, laid upon a planet fast losing her steam. You are barely a breath in the time space continuum, you're here, you're gone, we'd all move on without a care. You do not make an impact, you do not give or take anything of import in your ridiculous little life on this plastic earth. I am exactly what you think you see. I am indeed an actor human, paid in cash or credit or So Much Love and cookies to say these lines that a writer human wrote so that I might speak them in my actor human resonant voice, You are indeed the idiot that decided to pay to be squeezed in that little seat in the dark, for the next some hours of your life that you shall never retrieve, you may not take pictures or recordings, you must silence all cellphones beepers candy wrappers alarm clocks and all alarmedness in general, or we will tweet about you and your ignorance to the entire world during our greenroom smoke break, and you are exactly what you feel you are. That is the truth. Is that the truth?

You may think about this while some people are turning the noisy things off. Go on.

People turn their noisy things off.

The truth is a wobbly thing, we shall wobble through our own set of truths like jello on a freight train, and tonight I add a bump to that journey and put to you my truth:
I am not what you think you see.

And then again because three translates to God in bible, infinity in Asia, and funny in theater: I am the wolf.

Real wolf howl. Terrifying and beautiful.

I am the wolf. Aow.
yes, I am the wolf.
Aooow.

WOLF (cont)

Wolves get a bad rep for being evil, they will eat your lambs, limbs and grannies, and sometimes blow your house down without giving two shits about your chinny chin chin. But you gotta understand these evil wolves are abandoned wolves. Solo wolves, not necessarily out on the prowl to steal your red riding hoods. But stories need conflict, and fighters are sexy and boy, do wolves know how to fight.

Lights: Ash in the boxing ring

However, an abandoned wolf will rarely actually fight. He will slink in the shadows, trying his best to stay unseen and unheard and unsmelled, basically invisible. See, wolves suck at being alone. Wolves need family.

Lights: Robin and Ryan on couch with a blue balloon.

We sleep in packs. Hunt in packs. Travel in packs.

Lights: Peter in the car

The world is actually a very dangerous place, for an orphaned, lone wolf.

An Asian boy doll appears.

But I am the wolf. So I admit to some bias.

WOLF (cont)
There is a Korean saying that goes "Naturally, the arm folds inwards."
It means, you will tend to fight for your family, back your pack, defend your bloodline, over mostly anything and anyone else.
It makes more sense in Korean.
But we're not here to talk about Koreans.

"팔은 안으로 굽는다..."

Wolf sets the Asian boy doll in the car next to Peter.

We're here to talk about Americans.
These two Peters are both Americans. These two Peters live in the desert lands of Arizona.
Early one morning, the two American Peters opened the desert gate, and went out into the narrow desert road.

Sound: VRROOOM

Far down the road they travelled, over the hills and valleys low.
Until finally they came upon the great big jungle of shadows and concrete walls, The watery airs of San Francisco.
And in this jungle was a house, filled to the edges with blue balloons...

[Meet the Parents]

Ryan and Robin blow balloons.
Robin's balloon is very large.
It gets larger and larger. And just before it looks like it'll pop, it gets larger

RYAN

Are you trying to tell me something about the size of my balloons?

Robin takes in her village of blue balloons.

ROBIN

Did I overdo it?

RYAN

You? Overdo it? Whaaat? Nooo.

ROBIN

It's too much. It's trying too hard. I'm trying too hard.

RYAN

What's wrong with trying too hard?

ROBIN

What's wrong with trying too hard? There's nothing wrong with trying too hard, I Want him to know how hard I am trying and loving and wanting, to make him feel – What am I trying to make him feel?

[handwritten: Agree. I should be rewriting this scene to the grave]

RYAN

Like a person who is surrounded by very very many blue balloons.

ROBIN

I should've gotten yellow.

RYAN

Yellow balloons look like boobs. You don't wanna throw a three year old boy into a room full of boobs, do you?

ROBIN

I don't know Ryan, Okay? I don't know. Obviously maybe I don't know the first thing about what kind of room three year old boys like to get thrown into, okay?

RYAN

Hey hey, it was a joke. You do. You do know.

ROBIN

I do! I do know! I grew up with a perpetual 3 year old boy on the other side of my room. If anything I know too much!

RYAN

That's rude.

...

Where's Ash?

ROBIN

No idea.

RYAN

Woh. They're not coming? At all?

ROBIN

I don't know.

RYAN

I mean,

ROBIN

What.

RYAN

Can't blame them?

ROBIN

Can't blame them?!

RYAN

We're about to go pro, they've got a lot on their plate. You're dumping a kid on a person who's got no time / to sit around picking out balloon colors,

ROBIN

I am not dumping a kid on- You know what. I don't need you I don't need Ash I don't need any of you idiots, I am a goddamn adult I can goddamn get a child if I want.

RYAN

Okay.

They blow balloons.

RYAN

But if you really want my opinion on / this whole thing,

ROBIN

Oh my God.

RYAN

it's a little shady.

ROBIN

It's very legal.

RYAN

Oh come on, Robs, I can barely trust the internet to get a pair of jeans that fit, you just got yourself a kid, it's a little shady.

ROBIN

Jeans and children are very different things -

RYAN

You've never met the kid, or these people who put the kid up on a website, hello internet I hate this boy, yours for a couple of bucks if you'll sign this paper, we'll even throw in the basket of toys. Who does that?

ROBIN

Lots of people are doing it.

RYAN

Yeah you and the six people at clubs dot yahoo dot com

ROBIN

There are over a thousand members Ryan.

RYAN

On Clubs dot Yahoo dot Com, Robin – a thousand, ten thousand, whatever, it's still fucked up?

ROBIN

Why? Why is it so fucked up? Because we're bypassing some kind of institutional governmental system? Sure, coz they're so good at dealing with international orphans, so good that Russia, huh, has banned the US from adopting their children -

RYAN

Well no, that's because we do gay and they don't.

ROBIN

His room is done. We have balloons. My child is coming. So fuck you fuck Russia I do not have to convince either of you.

Ryan makes a balloon fart.

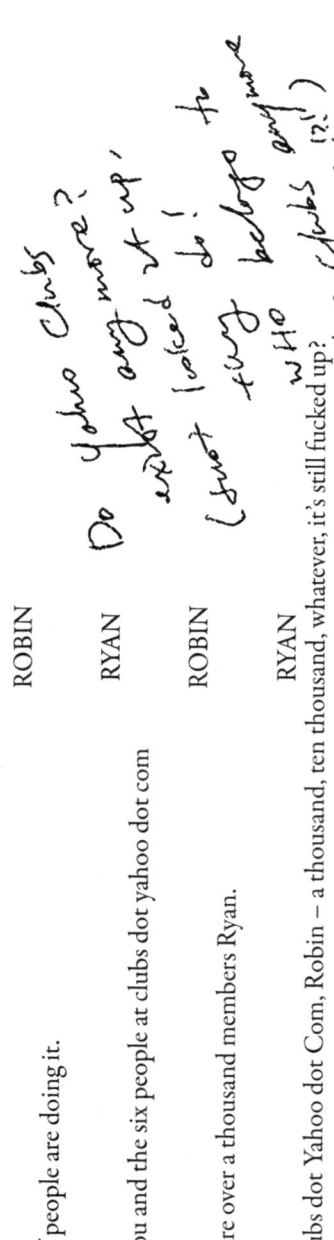

Sometimes I really wish you were a sister.

ROBIN

Sometimes I really wish you were a brother so, I guess (*sings, ala Wicked*) we deserve each other you and I ~

RYAN

Dustin *WTF*s *does not* buy that belting Wicked.

Ryan would start with him, I give you
if you agree permission to find
some other old song
that he learns the man to
your audience

ROBIN

Knock knock

He's here. Oh shit. Oh shit O Shit. Oshitoshitoshito

Robin does a last-minute-getting-things-perfect

I love the english language
for the things I get
to get away with
like saying the
whole phrase like it
is a word.

RYAN

Hey. Breathe.

She does.

RYAN (cont)

You got this. Okay?

ROBIN

Okay. I do. I do got this.

Knock knock

ROBIN

(to Ryan) Don't be dumb.

RYAN

--

She opens door.

Peter stands at the door with a large suitcase.
Next to him stands the Asian boy doll. Puppeteer is Wolf. Maybe Wolf and Doll look like Calvin and Hobbes in reverse.

ROBIN

Hi!

PETER

Hi I'm Peter.

Peter. Come in. Wonderful to meet you, I'm Robin.

ROBIN

Hi Robin. Excellent. And you must be Ash.

Ryan looks to Robin

PETER

This is Pete Junior.

Hey there Pete.

I'm Robin. I am so glad to finally meet you.

ROBIN
Directors thru the ages
have found this challenge
PETER
have to be established
first to establish who to carry while

PETER (cont)
- Door character said
- New character said
- Film to toy
- Baggage of this
- It's like this
- Times Nice

WOLF
I am a wolf.

ROBIN
—

WOLF
Wolves are not friendly in general. Especially the lone wolf.

ROBIN
THANK YOU DIRECTORS! :)
ALSO YOU ARE WELCOME

115

PETER

Junior wanna say hi to Robin and Ash?

WOLF

The wolf knows that he is alone, that all he has is his paws and his cunning to survive in the ever-changing environment.

PETER

He's tired. It's a tough drive,

ROBIN

Oh, yes. Of course.

WOLF

Wolves are never tired.
We just like to lay low. And watch.

PETER

Here, this is his / suitcase, it's mostly

ROBIN

Would you like anything to drink or, we have some snacks, Reese's Pieces, - unless you have a peanut allergy -, or dinner?

WOLF

Wolves are able to survive up to two weeks without food if need be.
Wolves are cautious, the masters of survival.

RYAN

We were going to order in some pizza –

ROBIN

Or there's a Great Korean place around the corner-

Wolf attacks a balloon. POP !!

WOLF

We know that every living being, even the tiniest and weak-looking-est has the potential of poison.

ROBIN

We were trying to decorate, festive, we got so excited, over-ballooned

PETER

No it's great, looks great. Junior likes blue.

ROBIN

Really? Oh wow, I didn't even know, it's like we connected on a subconscious level or something, I mean, not that a color of a balloon would indicate that we are Super Soul Mates or something, not that we should be, because we are not, we are I am just really very happy to have you. Here. Would you like some snacks, or Reese's, or something to drink? No?

PETER

He's shy. Takes a while to open up. But he will.

WOLF

We lay low. Observe. Calculate.

RYAN

He's kinda big for- how old you say he was?

ROBIN

Really quite big, you didn't look so grown up in your pictures! Do you play any sport? Basketball? Volleyball?

PETER

Sadly no he doesn't, I keep putting him in a team, any team, but the team spits him out, like a Canadian quarter.

Peter sets up a home-made tent.

PETER (cont)

Do you mind if I - ? It's his little fort. We made it together and he's a bit attached to it still.

ROBIN

Of course. Please.

PETER

It's not him, just that he is so shy and kids take a while to warm up sometimes

WOLF

It's highly unlikely that a wolf will bond with non-wolves.

PETER

It's a pity, he's very athletic. I mean especially for being Asian, I mean. It's a special quality. I mean, where we are from. I mean it in a good way. It could be different here, the city kids are open to a lot more, diversity and all that, so.

RYAN

Maybe we could try for a more individual sport, if team spirit is not his thing.

ROBIN

Yeh! He's a / trainer.

RYAN

I'm a trainer.

PETER

Trainer?

RYAN

Is that okay?

Handwritten marginalia:

I've always thought it funny to put things I know from white people's mouths back into the mouths of my white characters... a big time somewhere it stopped being funny and more enraging. But I left this here because I got used to the rhythm of the line...

PETER

No no, yes, no sorry, Katie said, that you were, made games.

ROBIN

Oh no it's me, that's me, I make video games. Or, work at a place, they make the games. I'm, I do stuff.

PETER

Yeah? Yeah yeah, that makes so much more sense, I mean, I was thinking, you have that build, like you do something with it,

RYAN

Have a club in the city, here.

Ryan gives Peter his card.

PETER

Oh. Aren't you-.

RYAN

Huh?

PETER

I thought your name was Ash.

RYAN

Oh. No. It's not.

PETER

Boxing?

RYAN

Mostly. We do some other stuff too, basic kickboxing,

PETER

That's actually pretty perfect. That would take the aggression out a bit

ROBIN

Oh.

PETER

Oh nothing, nothing unusual, just boys will be boys, kind of deal. He's really a good kid. Beautiful, when he wants to be. I mean, Katie and I, we had such a great time together, as a family,

WOLF

    Sometimes wolves will ally with another species for co-existence.
    Wolves are not above making friends if it means survival.

PETER

You must think I'm an animal, what kind of human being does this, but it's really, It's been hard with the baby, we have a newborn, we never thought we could, but anyway, he's, um, a lot to take care of. The baby, not-

WOLF

It's always about survival for the Lone Wolf

PETER

Junior's been having trouble with our split focus, and we love him so much, we love you so much, but he was just so unhappy. Katie was trying so hard.

WOLF

Sometimes you write a fine a realize with you have cracked an important part of the world was one fine this such

But wolves hate Katie.

PETER

I'm between jobs, which I thought it would help, but it turns out not.

WOLF

Katies hate Wolf.

PETER

And you have to know, when you're just not a good fit anymore, and,

WOLF

But Katies live with Peters

PETER

and we didn't know what to do.

WOLF

So even though Peters are very often allies, Peters are not hundred percent for the wolf.

PETER

This is his stuff, mostly clothes, some toys and uh, Katie and I wrote up a little thing, a booklet, we kept an observation log for the first few months. I typed it up. It's in the folder with the papers,

WOLF

Peters are a hundred percent for papers. It is his fortress of survival

ROBIN

Could I-

PETER

Yes yes of course.

ROBIN

Oh great. So it's been signed / and notarized

PETER

Absolutely. I keep a copy and you also

ROBIN

That's it? We don't need to go to court or

PETER

Yeah no that's it. I mean, technically this uh Power of Attorney contract is all it is, that's how people do it on the website. If we go to court he might slip into the cracks of the system, so it's just simpler, this way, it seems? And uh, affordable, a lot more.

WOLF

Peters love to talk about the cost of things.

ROBIN

Of course. I mean, that helps. Both of us.

PETER

Yeah children, you know. Cost.

WOLF

It seems to give him tremendous comfort to do so.

ROBIN

This is –

PETER
Yes, thanks. We also included some of his photos, when he was younger –

RYAN
Hey that's the one on the website,

PETER
Is it? Katie posted and kept up with all that stuff. I'm not-

ROBIN
He is six? Years old?

PETER
Yup.

ROBIN
O I thought,

PETER
Uh huh?

ROBIN
No, I was under the impression that he was younger, I thought I saw that on the post,

PETER

I'm pretty sure Katie wouldn't lie about,

WOLF

That is a lie. Katies lie all the time. She lies about her age, her weight, and what she ate for dessert.

PETER

Actually. There's one more thing we need to,

Another document

RYAN

What's that?

ROBIN

(*reads*) Affidavit of waiver of interest in child. Wow.

PETER

Since the POA doesn't transfer custody, technically, so we thought, just in case. You know?

ROBIN

Oh no I get it. Final sale, no returns?

PETER
We thought it would be best if, he would adjust better if we weren't around. At all.

WOLF
What?

PETER
We're really not terrible people. We really want what's best for him. We love him. So much. We do. It was wonderful to meet you.

Peter beads towards the door, the doll is attached to him.

Junior, Junior let go of daddy this is your new home now, okay?

WOLF
wolves are an extremely adaptable species / wolf is one of the few that survived the last ice age.

ROBIN
Junior, come on, wanna see your new room? We got a blue spaceship bed, and a whole new page of glow in the dark / planet stickers. We could help you stick them on your ceiling,

WOLF
pluck from the desert and throw into a sea a wolf will never drown a wolf will survive
But it takes TIME
It takes / TIME

127

RYAN

Hey hey, come on big boy, let's come to Uncle Ryan,

Doll is unattached from Peter. Ryan holds the doll. Wolf howl.

PETER

Um wait wait, you can't do that to him it'll just aggravate the tantrum

ROBIN

Tantrum? I think it's a little more than a tantrum,

PETER

Junior. Junior. Hey son, it's alright, huh, it's alright, it's
Be a big boy for daddy? Huh? Everything's gonna be alright okay? Everything's gonna be just fine. You gotta be a big boy right now, okay? I love you, so much, you know that right? You know -

*Door slam. Ash is home.
Wolf stops howling.*

PETER

Oh! Hi I, I'm Peter.

*Peter holds out his hand.
It hangs there in the air.
It's awkward.*

ASH

You're the dad.

PETER

Um, yes. Well, I was. legally at this / point I might not-

ASH

I hope you go to hell.

PETER

Woah.

ASH

Get the fuck out of my house.

PETER

I don't think that kind of language is necessary

ASH

Get your ass the fuck out of my house or I'll throw you out the window like your mother should've done.

RYAN

Hey, come on let's let the man go, okay?

ASH
Did I say anything but? I said get out. Get out. Get the fuck out of my house.

PETER
How about you back off, alright? I didn't drive all the way down here to be disrespected by some,

ASH
By some?

PETER
I don't know who you are but you have absolutely no right to talk to me that way.

ASH
Yeah?

PETER
You just watch your mouth, alright? The kid is just six.

ASH
We can import him from Asia, we can put him up for auction the minute something doesn't Feel Right, but hey now be careful of the f word coz that will really fuck him up.

ROBIN
Ash. That's enough.

The GAY AGENDA

PETER
Ash? You are Ash.

ASH
?

PETER
You're-. You are the-. *(to Ryan)* You, know about this? Did you know this, that

RYAN
Hey look man,

PETER
(to Robin) Does Katie know? Did you lie about,

ROBIN
I'm sorry, did I lie about what?

PETER
She would never just,

RYAN
Peter I think you better leave now,

131

The GAY RAGE

PETER
He won't have a father? You're depriving my boy of a father?

ROBIN
Wow okay I'm sorry but if anyone's depriving / him of anything it's

RYAN
Ash no don't,

Ash punches him in the face

AAAAAAAAAARRRRGH, / ARHG!

PETER
Ash Calm it, okay, just not worth it.

RYAN
crazy fucking bitch!

PETER
Careful what you say now.

RYAN

Wolf Prompt #1
Write a scene where being absent about someone who as someone talked into comes does anything slowly unnoticed to j.

PETER

She punched me!

RYAN

Do you need some ice for that?

PETER

What? No I don't need

RYAN

Then close the door on your way out.

Peter leaves.

RYAN

The fuck was that?

ASH

Go home Ryan.

RYAN

Where the hell were you? You can't just disappear and appear and punch a guy in the face like that, they have a place for people who do that it's called prison.

Ash looks to puppet.

ASH

What's your name?

ROBIN

Peter. His name's Peter.

ASH

Hey kid what's your name?

ROBIN

Ash.

The wolf growls.

RYAN

Ash, lay off, you're scaring him.

Ash crouches down to meet Puppet's eyes.
The wolf growls.

Whether or not
you can see the eyes
of a stage performer
Always makes a difference
in a play.
But I find it to
absolutely essential
in this play.
(I'll never go to broadway.
I shall now endeavor to
write plays where
EYES matter less)

You okay over there?

ASH

The wolf growls, lunges at Ash.
Ash catches his arms. Gentle but firm, like a coach guiding a punch.
But the boy's fist is odd.
His arms are weird too. And his chest, legs, ...face.
Behind the puppet, Ash is surprised to find Wolf's eyes.

Wolf growls come to an abrupt, equally surprised stop.
Ash removes the puppet from between them,
And stands up to meet Wolf
A mix of the familiar with the terribly unexpected.

Huh.

ASH

Ash looks to the puppet, to the wolf, to the puppet -
Wolf snatches the puppet back.

135

HOOOOOOOOOOWWWWWWWWL!

Wolf recovers.

WOLF

Contrary to popular belief, wolves do not howl at the full moon any more often than at other shapes of the moon. They do, however, howl more during the sunset and sunrise – during the change of light.

Light changes.

[night]

ROBIN
Done. Took two hours, five stories, three repeats, but the kid is finally asleep. None of it helped, I don't think. He just exhausted himself, crying. But hey, it's done, we finally have a sleeping child in our child sleeping bed. Wanna come see? I keep having this urge to go peek at him sleeping. Is that super predatory or super parental? Ash. Ash? Hey, you awake?

ASH

Real Question to Real Parents...?

It's late.

ROBIN
No it's not. Come let's go look at him, kids are great when they're conked out.
You know you want to...

ASH
I don't.

ROBIN
Okay I know you're still, not on board with this, but he's here now. He'll know if you're not on board, he'll know if you don't like him. Please like him. Or just pretend-like him. Pretend will become present, present will become past, and it'll be like you've known and loved him all your life. Ash, come on. Talk to me.

ASH
I don't want to talk right now.

137

ROBIN
Then when? When do you wanna talk about it, when he goes to college? Coz that's gonna come around real -

ASH
Oh My God Robin will you Let me Sleep.

ROBIN
I just think we should talk. While he is asleep.

ASH
didn't cross your mind to "talk" before you went and bought a kid off Facebook?

ROBIN
Yahoo. And we did talk

ASH
And I said no.

ROBIN
You said you would think about it.

ASH
Robs, I really don't want to deal with this right now

ROBIN

When do you ever want to deal with anything?
I'm so happy about this, Ash. I really am.
I'm sorry I couldn't wait for you to be done thinking about it,
for someone's unaffordable sperm to catch my sad shriveled eggs but right now there's a child, in our house,
can we please just be grown ups about this?

ASH

This is grown up? Getting a child from Yahoo? You're pissed coz I won't deal with you wanting to get a child from Yahoo?

ROBIN

I know it wasn't the / best way to go about it but

ASH

like a pet, like some kind of second hand toy?! I have my pro debut in a couple months, I'm stressed the fuck out, and then this -
So I won't sacrifice my whole life and body to your needs, I'm the asshole

ROBIN

I never asked you / to sacrifice

ASH

No. You didn't ask. You just went and did and reported.

ROBIN

Okay I fucked up.
He was there.
And nobody wanted him.
You were thinking, for so long,
And I kept -,
I was lingering at the toy aisles,
watched back to back episodes of power rangers
shy Korean boy with beautiful smile eager to please loves power rangers, the posting said,
I couldn't stop reading his post. I've memorized that post.
And I just had to, if nothing else, I had to get him off the internet.
I called them to see, just to see if he was still there
but he was still there and they were so,
quick,
everything happened so fast and
I fucked up. I'm sorry.
Be mad at me, not at him.

ASH

I'm not mad at him I dont know him Robin I can't feel stuff for a stranger overnight.

ROBIN

I know.

140

ASH

I can't develop an attachment to someone just coz he lives in my house now. I've barely developed an attachment to myself.

ROBIN

Not asking you to feel anything overnight. I'm asking you to come look at a sleeping child with me. That is all I ask.

ASH

Fine.

ROBIN

Yes? Yes! Okay but you have to be real quiet, you have no idea how hard it was to - (off Ash's look) We go.

WOLF

Wolves use different locations for rest.

ASH

This is the weirdest stupidest,

ROBIN

Shhh...

WOLF
dens are usually constructed for pups, to protect them from natural dangers of the wild.

ASH
I'm not gonna fall in love with him over a

ROBIN
Ash shut up you're gonna wake him. Isn't he great?

ASH
Yeah.

WOLF
Wolves are very territorial.

Wolf squeezes a bottle of water on the puppet

ROBIN
Wait what is this smell?

ASH
What smell?

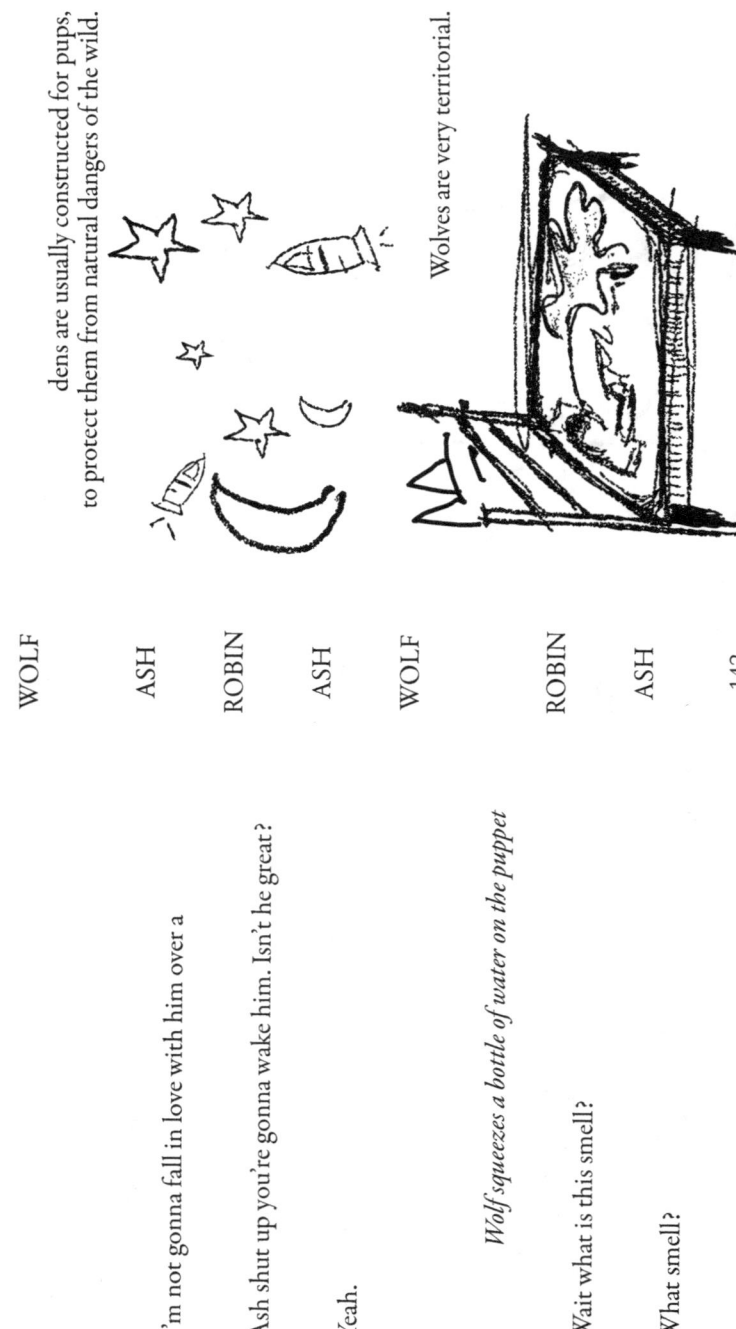

ROBIN

It's like,

WOLF

And so the wolf uses scent to mark territory.

ASH

Oh wow.

ROBIN

I've never seen it actually happen before.
I mean, in real time, happening before me.

WOLF

However, captive wolves have even been known to urinate in strange places, such as ponds and streams - to confuse potential enemies.

ROBIN

Should we wake him up? I mean we can't let him sleep like this? Do people just let their kids sleep in pee?

ASH

I don't think most people know coz most people don't spy on their kids while they are sleeping.

ROBIN

Well I did, and now I know, and now I'm gonna be the mom who knew and left her kid to roll around in his own pee.

ASH

Have fun mom. I'm going to bed.

Ash leaves.

[Daily Life]

WOLF

The habitats of wolves can be found in areas that you may not ever imagine them surviving. In the arctic, in the swamps, deserts, caves, ... kitchens,

A familiar kitchen / dining area

Ash runs in from morning run, gulps some water

WOLF

Give them a place to eat, a place to play, and a place to rest and any wolf pack will be okay.

Ryan enters with his earphones in.
Same space, different place.

Ash leaves to take a shower.

Ryan gets bacon and eggs from fridge gets his morning routine going.

Robin enters, carrying her purse.

ROBIN

Ash? Ash, are you back?

No answer, but the shower's running.

ROBIN

I'm getting some things for breakfast. Wait to eat, Ok?

Phone rings. Ryan clicks earphones.

RYAN

Mom! Hold up.

Ryan spits to basin, runs water, wipes mouth.

RYAN

Good morning, how you doing?

*Peter enters
Same space, different place.*

Peter gets a saucepan, fills it with water, puts it on stovetop.

Robin writes a message for Ash

RYAN

Yeah I saw him.
Was there almost all night.
I don't know, he looks like what Asian kids look like, like an Asian kid.
Nah, way older. Six.

Of course it's insane. Tried what I could, but you know, Stubborn Robin.

Robin sticks note on fridge, leaves.

Ha, no. She didn't know either.
She thought he was three.
She got punked, you know, what you gonna expect from the internet.

No, no, we didn't press it with the father

Peter opens fridge, looks,

PETER

Katie?
Katie, where'd you put the milk?

Peter closes fridge, opens freezer, looks,

No, not in the freezer either.

It's alright I got it, but it's ok to mix formula with breast feeding? Yeh, okay.

Wolf and puppet sit at kitchen table.

RYAN

There was no time to ask, the kid was crying like a siren

Yes he was crying,

it's a new house with new people,

everything was blue and,

Listen Mom why don't you talk to her yourself,

Does she even know you know that they adopted?

Peter makes the baby formula by mixing powder with cold water and sticking bottle in the pot of water as it gets heated (it's wrong, but it's how he does it)

PETER

Honey, do you have the email, of those people that you found?

I thought we should check in to see -

No I'm not being clingy

I just wanted to check in to-

Because you never told me they were-.

It's okay Never mind.

I said never mind

RYAN

Jesus -

PETER

Katie it's fine it was just a question, okay?

Peter disappears to the unseen Katie.

RYAN

You guys have some issues to sort out. Just give her a call! I feel like the fucking Wimbledon ball boy running back and forth between you two.

Ryan disappears with Bacon and Eggs and Phone

Wolf and puppet sit at kitchen table.

Ash, back in kitchen after a shower.

Ash gets out bowl, spoon, cereal… catches wolf sitting, staring at them.
Freeze.

A weird form of silent showdown.

ASH

Robs? Robin you up?

Puppet and Wolf continue to stare at Ash.

Ash finds post-it, chucks it in the trash.
Ash pours themself some cereal, milk,

Puppet and Wolf continue to stare at Ash.
Ash stares back for a while.

Then they find another bowl, spoon, gets two boxes of cereal.

ASH
Want some? We got lucky pops and... Organic Multigrain Square, from Kashi.

Puppet and Wolf continue to stare at Ash.

ASH

Have a preference?

Puppet and Wolf continue to stare at Ash.

Ash pours both kinds into the bowl, hands the breakfast to the kid. Back to reading. Ash eats. Wolf picks up a spoon.

ASH

You're a lefty, huh?

Wolf changes the spoon to his right hand

ASH

Me too.

Ash holds up their spoon. In their left hand.

ASH

It's the cooler hand. No one can see it coming.

Cautiously, Wolf changes back to left hand. They eat.

WOLF

Jeenu.

ASH

Huh?

WOLF

My name.

ASH

Jeenu.

Puppet nod.

Enter Ryan. He puts empty plate and fork into sink, rinses etc.

RYAN
Their name is Ash mom.
They've been married to Robs for- I really wish you'd get over this.

Robin with groceries

ROBIN
Good morning! Who's up for some Eggs Florentine, huh?

ASH
I'm good.

ROBIN
Oh. You didn't get my note?

ASH
I did.

ROBIN
Oh.

...

Pete?

Wolf and puppet stop eating cereal. Looks to Ash. Looks to Robin.

RYAN
Alright. I'll tell her you said so.

Peter rushes in

PETER
Oh fuck me.

Peter squirts the bottle contents on his wrist to check temperature. It's hot. Ow.

Ow!

Ok. I won't.

ROBIN
That's okay, maybe tomorrow then.

Ding! Like the end of a round of boxing.

[Play-Fight]

WOLF
Wolf packs rarely succeed in adopting other wolves into their fold,

RYAN
Chin down, kid,

WOLF
Discovered loners are typically killed,

RYAN
you're all open,

WOLF
eviscerated,

RYAN
Ryan taps puppet on cheek

See? And then you're out. Guard up. Guard up.

Wolf's guard is up

A new wolf will be challenged to fight to secure a place in the hierarchy

The WOLF RAGE

WOLF	
RYAN	Uh uh, no kicking buddy, just the fists one two one two
WOLF	and will undoubtedly shift the order of things
ROBIN	Easy Ryan,
RYAN	Guard up!
	Taps puppet in the face, Wolf growls.
ROBIN	Okay that's enough.
RYAN	He needs to be a little more assertive.

ROBIN

He needs to not be punched in the face is what he needs. Come here, you okay? Pete?

RYAN

He's fine. You really shouldn't coddle him Robin.

ROBIN

He's six.

RYAN

Robs, it's like a jungle out there for boys like him. We gotta prep little Peetie, for when he's out there, gotta stand up for himself like one of Uncle Ryan's boys, right Pete?

ASH

Jeenu.

ROBIN

What's that?

ASH

Name's not Pete. It's Jeenu.

ROBIN How'd you know?

ASH He said his name was Jeenu.

ROBIN He said that?

RYAN It speaks!

ROBIN The papers didn't say–

ASH Yehwell, the papers is wrong.

ROBIN Hey wait, when? What else did he say?

ASH Nothing, I asked if he wanted cereal, he said his name was Jeenu, I said cool and we ate some cereal.

RYAN
Alright round two, Ding, round's started, kid, guard up, guard up,

ROBIN
Why didn't you tell me?

ASH
Thought you knew.

ROBIN
Why? Why would I go on calling him not his name if I knew that wasn't what he-

ASH
Okay, chill, now we know.

ROBIN
United front, Ash, we agreed on united front

ASH
I don't even know what that is, so, no, we didn't agree on -

Another punch to the face, Puppet growls.

ROBIN

Ryan what is the matter with you?

Robin holds puppet while Wolf growls, circles Ryan, lay low.

RYAN

Hey you're the one who asked me for the favor.

WOLF

ROBIN

Okay well you suck at this.

RYAN

Some of these kids, you just gotta knock 'em down to get them out of their shells, okay? Just send him over to the club with Ash

ROBIN

Ha, yeah that's not happening

WOLF

observe, calculate,

RYAN

It's not good for him to have his mom all over his face

WOLF

we know to wait for the time to ...

Wolf leaps on Ryan

RYAN

OWW! You little shit you little fucking little shit

Wolf continues to beat up Ryan, in a small vicious way that animals do

ROBIN

Pete- Jeenu. That is not nice, you don't ambush people when they are not ready, / that is not what

RYAN

Kid's got a little asshole behind all the pussy.

ROBIN

Ryan please. Jeenu did you hear what I said? Look at me please,
if you want to throw a punch, train at the gym and follow the rules. We are not animals.

WOLF

I'm a wolf.

ROBIN

ogize? say I'm sorry? Pete- Jeenu. It's not okay to hurt people like how you just hurt Uncle Ryan.

WOLF

I'm a lone wolf

ROBIN

I'm a lone wolf I have to protect myself

WOLF

ROBIN

Pet- fu-. Sorry, Jeenu. Look at me please?

Hello? Anyone there?

Wolf howls. Attacks Robin.
Ryan holds puppet. Wolf howls and growls

RYAN

That's got to not ever happen again, or I'm gonna fucking fuck you up, alright?

ROBIN

Ryan! Turn it off.

RYAN

You don't lay a finger on your mom, do you understand me, I asked you a question.

ROBIN

He's six. There's a limit to the damage he can do.

RYAN

He's six. You keep saying that like it's like some safety net,

Ryan puts him down

ROBIN

Safety net from what? No one is falling Ryan.

RYAN

I'm telling you there are some seriously fucked up six year old boys out there, okay?

Ash walks up to wolf,

Wolf slugs at them but they jump back.

ASH
Keep that up you'll be wrung out by round two. Right foot forward. No, right foot, coz you're a southpaw, lefty right? Like that,

Ash places wolf's right foot in front and turns his body

He slugs again and Ash jumps back,

ASH
Uh uh, not yet. Gotta lay low, lay low,
Observe, calculate,

WOLF
Observe, calculate!

Somehow the puppet is gone.

ASH
Coz you don't know how they gonna fight, do you?
Light on your feet, scouting for an in, right? Up up up

*Ash jump-jump-jumps lightly
Wolf emulates.*

ASH

Good, that's very good,
right foot forward so you got the distance to run back when you need to keep jumping gotta keep light, jump jump, left hand at your ear like you're on the phone, hello?

JEENU

Hello.

ASH

That's right One two, one two, good One two, one two, good good
Okay but if you're fighting against orthodox, right handers,
They're gonna be coming fast, coz the distance is shorter,
See, / comes at you real fast,
So what do you do? Side step, like this, one two shift, one two shift, right?
Okay one two shift, one two ...

Wolf watches, mesmerized.

WOLF

Pups of a pack will "play-fight" with each other,
forming a hierarchy at the kids' tables.
The hierarchy will shift with the development of the pup, as he matures into a grown up wolf, as a member of the pack.

[Finding Footing]

Phone rings. Machine click

RYAN

Thank you for calling Ryan's Den Boxing Club the official boxing club of the cub. Our office is currently closed. Please leave a message after the beep or call back during our official business hours:

PETER

Hi, this is Peter Hunt, I don't know if you remember me, we met briefly when I dropped off Junior at your house. Or, rather, not sure if it was your, anyway, I wanted to thank you for being there, to help out with the negotiations that night, I think we all could have handled the situation a little better, me included, so. I do realize that we had agreed that there would be no contact from our end but, well that is why I didn't call to the house, or attempted to reach them.
I had some concerns, regarding, I found your card, you know that you gave me and so. I had some questions regarding Junior's adjustments, and well, quite frankly How he is responding to having a,
two moms.
And so
I thought I would call to see, to um, reach out to you, since we did meet before. Again, Peter Hunt, you can reach me at this number. Thank you.

During message: Ryan and Ash in the ring.

AT THE

• • • •

RYAN

Alright stop. what the hell Ash.

ASH

Fuhhhhck.

RYAN

We're weeks away from the fight, you can't afford to shit away time like this.

ASH

Sorry. A little off. A little off today.

RYAN

It's not-.

ASH

What.

RYAN

It's not just today.

ASH

Sorry. I'm distracted

RYAN
You a smarts boxer not a power boxer, gotta keep your head in the ring. Hundred and ten percent.

ASH
Mm hmm.

RYAN
Tommy Tavarez has never been in a ring with a Southpaw. He's got no clue how to fight you, Ash. He'll see that left hook and be like woah, what? Bam down. We really have a chance at winning your debut. Real prize money. Ker-ching right?

ASH
Yeh yeh.

RYAN
Ash.

ASH
Mm?

RYAN
Are you with me?

ASH
Sorry. Yes. God, I'm just all over the place.

RYAN

Do I have to worry?

Ash shrugs.

How's stuff at home.

ASH

You know. Robs is insane busy, even with the maternity leave from her work, there's the school stuff, the shrink stuff, and she's trying to get him into Yoga, He's so quiet most times but then we're getting calls about broken windows, goldfish bowls, other kids' noses…
The other day we got called in coz he glued his eyes shut with bubble gum. He's something, the kid.

RYAN

Yeh, he's a bit not so ordinary.

ASH

He's a freak a bit, but smart, I think.
They said he's at least two grade levels above his age group in comprehension and fine motor skills, as well as

Ash laughs

RYAN

What?

ASH

I was just thinking, that time when you tried to teach him boxing, he beat the crap outta you? He's not a natural by any means, not what I'm saying, he's definitely not the build, a little demented- He, kinda reminds me of when I was a kid. I was kinda demented.

RYAN

Was?

ASH

Yeah shut the fuck up.

RYAN

It's a compliment. I like my fighters slightly deranged. Feral. Gr.

ASH

Yup.

RYAN

But in the ring, right? Be feral in the ring. Gotta be ferally focused, k? Grr.

ASH

You know, I was thinking.

RYAN

?

ASH

No it's just, there's so much going on, I feel so ungrounded,

RYAN

I can see that, that's why I'm / saying you gotta

ASH

And I'm wondering if we should, cancel.

RYAN

Cancel.

ASH

Or, postpone.

RYAN

-

ASH

I know I know I know, it was real hard to get this bout, and I appreciate everything you've done to make shit happen, but you told me to tell you if I feel like I'm not ready and you know, I feel like-

RYAN

You are.

ASH

Come on, I'm a mess Ry.

RYAN

So you wanna cancel.

ASH

Or postpone, if we / can.

RYAN

No. Don't do this. You are not doing this to me.

ASH

To you? What am I doing to you? It's my ass getting whupped up there if I'm not ready

RYAN

So Be Ready! Be fucking ready!

RYAN (cont)
Do you understand - your career, should you choose to have it, could change the game forever -

ASH
What if I am not interested in changing –

RYAN
What if it's not all about you or what you are fucking interested in? You wanted to fight a fucking dude for your pro debut that you could've killed two years ago fighting a chick, You wanted this, I said yes to you I made that happen I have been making it happen five years now. Look. I know I was never gonna top it like you are gonna top it and I am Happy to be in your shadow, in your corner, I've been there, haven't I? You're not gonna throw in the towel on our five years. Ash.

ASH
Okay.

RYAN
Cancel, postpone, can't be saying shit like that.

ASH
Alright.

RYAN
We're a team. One boat. What you do is what I've done.

ASH

Yeah. Yeah okay. I get it. Sorry.

Back to the ring.
Phone rings. Machine click

RYAN

Thank you for calling Ryan's Den Boxing Club the official boxing club of the cub. Our office is currently closed. Please leave a message after the beep or call back during our official business hours:

PETER

Ryan, hi this is Peter, I just wondered if you got my message....s. I don't want to hound you, if that's not what you're about, but I just wanted make sure I'm calling the right guy, or that I'm getting through, you might have a, unstable intern situation or. I don't know why I said that. Anyway, I'd really love an update of any kind. On Junior. Pete. Thanks. Bye.

Click.

WOLF

Peters tend to worry too much. This is because he doesn't understand,

WHO INTERNS AT:

LION'S DEN
RYAN SHEPHERD
C.E.O. COACH

PETER WANTS TO KNOW

[Daily Life 2]

A familiar kitchen / dining area

                WOLF

... wolves are an extremely adaptable species. They can survive in the arctic, in the swamps, deserts, caves, ... kitchens,

Ash runs in from morning run, gulps some water, earphones in.

                WOLF (cont)

You get the picture.

    Ryan enters, brushing teeth, earphones in.

    Ash goes to shower

    Ryan gets bacon and eggs from fridge, frying pan on stovetop.

    Phone rings.

RYAN
Mom!
Good morning to you too.
Oh, um, haven't been over there for a while. Been busy. I told you, our club's first pro bout-

ROBIN
Ash? Wait to eat, okay?

Robin leaves.

No Mom, I did tell you, but whatever
Alright, well I'll keep telling you till you remember, I'm nothing if I don't keep you from going senile.
Whatever, you love me.

He's fine, I guess. She's fine. They're all fine, no one's burnt the house down just yet.

Peter enters

Peter gets a saucepan, fills it with water, puts it on stovetop, opens fridge, looks,

PETER
Oh come on. Seriously?

Peter opens freezer, looks,

PETER
Katie, we're out again.

RYAN

You're just waiting for something to go wrong so you can wag your finger at them.

I'm kidding!

Mom it was joke, okay?

Geez, lighten up a little.

They're managing fine, she got some kind of maternity leave, stupid if you ask me

Well because the boy is six! I don't see other moms with six year olds getting paid to stay home?

Peter Slams both fridge and freezer door.

PETER

Yes we are.

You know honey, if you don't wanna do something, just don't start it?

I really don't give a shit about formula or breast milk, just pick one and commit to it you know? Can we do that? Can we fucking commit to one fucking thing, for a change?

Yeh well it's hard for me too for us both okay?

Seriously?

176

RYAN
Yeah, he's still wetting his bed, apparently kid's got issues.

PETER
Don't talk to me like that. Don't fucking, yeh? Really?

I did not!
You're remembering wrong, I didn't,

Okay well I'm sorry but fucking fuck / fuck fuckitty fucking fuckfuckfuck.

Okay that's enough, fun is over,

You want to do this? Let's do this.

Ryan disappears with Bacon and Eggs and Phone

Peter leaves.

Wolf and puppet sit at kitchen table.

Ash gets out two bowls, two spoons, milk...

And the two boxes of cereal

ASH
Pops? Kashi?

Puppet and Wolf shrug.
Ash pours the cereal, milk, hands one bowl to Wolf, sits on the counter, opens something to read. They eat.
Wolf pulls out something to read too. Maybe about wolves. He eats. Ash notices his little book. Maybe Ash finds it funny. Wolf and puppet look up at them. Did he do something wrong? Ash goes back to their reading.

Wolf continues to look at them.

WOLF
Where do you go every morning?

ASH
Running.

WOLF
From?

ASH
What do you mean?

WOLF
What are you running from?

ASH

Nothing, I'm just running. Sometimes around the park, sometimes down the pier.

WOLF

Why?

ASH

Just, I don't know. It's a nice way to start a day. My ritual, you know?

WOLF

Can I come with?

ASH

Oh. Um. Well, it's kind of a solo thing, buddy. And I run very fast. And you'll have to get up very early.

WOLF

I am always awake before you are.

ASH

Yeah? Having trouble sleeping?

WOLF

No. And I am fast. I am faster than you.

ASH
We'll see about that tomorrow morning.

Enter Ryan. He puts empty plate and fork into sink, rinses etc.

RYAN
Jeenu. It's Korean. It's a Korean name. I don't know mom, no one gives a shit whether he's bilingual or not.

Robin enters, sees cereal party

ROBIN
Oh come on.

ASH
What.

ROBIN
I said I was making pancakes.

ASH
I can't do pancakes right now.

Peter is back.

PETER
Fuck this.

ROBIN

Jeenu? Do you want-

Wolf and puppet stop eating cereal. Looks to Ash. Looks to Robin.

ROBIN

That's okay, I'll make some for me.

RYAN

God can we stop talking about this kid already, I'd think he had a platinum penis the way all of you gab on about him.

What. I can say penis to my mom I'm a grown man. Penis penis penis pe- Hello? Mom?

PETER

You make the formula. I'm going for a walk.

Ding! Like the end of a round of boxing.

[Sometimes Allies]

Ryan's gym. Peter enters.

RYAN

We're closing down for the weekend, sorry man. Oh. THIS SCENE

PETER

Hi.

RYAN

Okay.

PETER

Nice space. It's very, spacious.

RYAN

You're the guy.

PETER

The guy. Who sold his kid on the internet. Yes. I am him.

RYAN

What do you want?

PETER

I just thought, you gave me your card. I left, um, on your machine. You weren't responding to my messages.

RYAN

No coz you're the guy who sold his kid on the internet.

PETER

Right.

RYAN

So what the fuck do you want?

PETER

I wanted, well, to get more diapers.

RYAN

Because we were running out and Katie's not very future oriented at the moment. And then I missed my exit thinking about how Katie is not very future oriented or hasn't been ever really and I just kept driving, thinking about things like that. And got here. So I thought I would

182

PETER (cont)
come by. To see if you had gotten my messages. Which you have. And so. Now. I'll, leave. Sorry.

Peter turns to leave.

RYAN
Hey. What are you doing, man.

PETER
I don't know.

RYAN
You gotta stop. Can't leave me messages, can't come around like this, it's not right.

PETER
I miss him. I miss him a lot.

RYAN
So then why did you do it?

PETER
I don't know. I was underslept, and Katie was crying all day, the baby was crying all day, I kept thinking something had to give something had to change, and we changed the wrong thing. I think we changed the wrong thing. But if he's doing good. I have no right to miss him. I've had my chance I've had my run and I fucked it up I get that. But I just wanted to make sure that he is okay. Then I can move on, you know? I can just focus on my life and my family. Is he? Okay?

RYAN
Yeah. Sure. I mean, there are some issues, at school and stuff, like with windows, and goldfish bowls, he's apparently super smart, they're taking him to a shrink and yoga

PETER
Yoga? He likes Yoga?

RYAN
You know what, I don't know. If you wanna check up on the kid, I'm not that guy. He's not here.

PETER

I thought of going to the house but

RYAN

Why didn't you?

PETER

I just need to know he's okay.

RYAN

Kid's got issues, it's gonna be bumpy but he's not your problem anymore.

PETER

He was never a problem. Are they treating him as a problem? He's aggressive sometimes, but it's just boys will be boys kind of thing, they don't understand, see this is what I'm talking about.

RYAN

Okay no don't talk about my family like you know them, you don't. They aren't treating him like anything that he is not and even if they are you do not have a say in any of this do you understand?

PETER

How is he taking to you?

RYAN

What?

PETER

Does Junior, does he take to you? Listens?

RYAN

Sure, yeah.

PETER

And you, you are around a lot at the place, right? Do you, you get along with Junior?

RYAN

Peter. You did a shitty-ass thing and it is eating at you, I get it. Good news is, you lucked the fuck out in finding my sister. Kid is surrounded by people who want him to come out on top.

A. CB3 Sheila and Sarah said I could!! LOL3

No.

I've always felt like this scene doesn't belong in the play. Took it out, put it back in, dozens of times...

Claustrophobic, upsetting, void of magic, lacking play...

I wanted it to look and feel different.

PETER
Ok. That's all I wanted to know.

Ok. Thank you.

PETER
But you,

RYAN
I am around a lot at the place.

(D) MHM!! IN ONLY COMMAS IN THIS SCENE???

[Who's your favorite, mommy or mommy?]

Wolf shadow boxing in his fantasy world. Puppet is chucked away somewhere else.

WOLF
A new wolf will be challenged to fight, for his place in the order of things.
And the omega wolves of the pack (like dumbass Ryan) will feel threatened.
The omega wolves (like dumbass Ryan) will do anything to put the new wolf in his place.

Ash walks by, and sees Wolf.
Wolf notices Ash but pretends to not notice,

WOLF (cont)
But the new wolf will put up a great fight. Because the wolf is a fighter. Up, up, up, he is light on his feet, scouting for an in, Super on the phone, talking on the phone I'm like, hello, hello? That's right, hello.

Robin walks in on the secret intimacy,

ROBIN
Jeenu! In a Gym, with gloves and a grown up, okay? Come on, do you have your Yoga things ready?

Wolf immediately turns back to puppet.

ASH

Why yoga?

ROBIN

Oh, hey babe, didn't see you there. He likes it.

ASH

Six year old boys don't do yoga, usually

[handwritten: could MATCH tempo & move scene #2 Do this forever]

ROBIN

Well. He does, Right Jeenu.

WOLF

ROBIN

I'm just waving a stick in the dark here, see if I can strike something. If nothing else, it's a nice bonding event for us, right champ?

WOLF

Wolves hate yoga.

ROBIN

I'd ask you to come, but you're not into that sort of

WOLF

Wolves hate yoga.

ASH

Yeh, I can't be seen with my ass in the public air,

ROBIN

We're gonna go to In-N-Out later if you wanted to come-

ASH

God no, Ryan would kill me, still have three pounds to lose before the fight next week.

ROBIN

Yeah, how is all that going?

ASH

Fine. It's fine.

ROBIN

Are you feeling-

ASH

It's fine. Anyways, I was on my way to the club so. You guys have fun.

ROBIN

See you later.

WOLF

Can I go to the club with Ash?

ROBIN

Oh. But we were gonna go to In-N-Out after, remember? You don't wanna do that?

ASH

I can take him, I don't mind. If you're coming with me, be ready in two minutes coz I'm late.

Wolf and puppet run off.

ROBIN

I mean, it's just exercise, but if you don't want to, that's fine, I guess.
I'm sure I can get a refund for the rest of the sessions.

ASH

Okay.

ROBIN

Okay.

ASH

Are you? Okay?

ROBIN

I'm fine.

ASH

I can't do the passive aggressive nodding decoding, you know that right? Shoot straight, Robs.

ROBIN

No it's fine. I'm sorry.

ASH

Cool. ... Jeenu? Tick tock tick tock kid let's go!
I'm gonna go start the car, bring him out when's he ready?

ROBIN

Okay actually no. I can't do this, I feel like the fucking maid, popping around doing chores while you're the one getting any kind of real Anything out of him, I barely know the sound of his voice, until you're there, and he's all like, hi my name is not the name you thought it was and you're like cool, okay, and you "forget" to tell me, just like you "forget" that I told you I wanted to make breakfast for us and you "forget" I asked you to wait till I got back and you "forget" to make it to the appointments with Dr. Schneider and so Jeenu thinks I'm the evil boring mom while you're the cool boxing mom. Meanwhile you don't do the laundry you don't do the groceries you don't pick up his tens of thousands of tiny toys you

ROBIN (cont)
keep loading down on him every time you go for a "hangout" at IKEA, while you conveniently forget things that make you the not-cool mom.

ASH

Okay.

ROBIN

No! Not okay. It's not fair to think like this, if he's good with you, and happy, I should be happy too but I'm not. If he hates yoga and likes to punch people I have to step back and let him be him and be proud but I don't know how to not want the things I want first.

ASH

What do you want.

ROBIN

A child.

ASH

He is one.

ROBIN

Or someone who eats some meals of the week with me or I don't know, look my way and talk to me about things they are feeling and maybe wants to go to yoga with me because my wife clearly can't be doing any of -

ASH

Don't make this about me, Robs.

ROBIN

You didn't even want him in the first place,

ASH

Okay wow that helps nothing. This is, I can't. I have to go I'm late. Take him to yoga.

ROBIN

You can't just leave you promised Jeenu you would take him to the club

ASH

Robin Oh my god!

WOLF

Wolves do not need Yoga.

ROBIN

Hey you. When d'you sneak back. You have your jacket?

Puppet nods.

ASH

I have to go.

ROBIN

Make sure he keeps his jacket on. He's had a little cough lately, I've noticed

Ash and Wolf leave.

Ash comes back.

ASH

You do not get to blame this on me, sit in your sad corner and make me feel bad, You fucked Me up. I'm about to go pro, Robin, have a shot at being something real.
But this thing this person is taking over my head space my life space,
I have a six year old with me on my morning run which is now a walk and, Fuck I like it I actually love it and it is really not great time to be loving anything else but the ring, but I could give two shits about the ring and this has never happened before and its scary and I am not ready and its your fault and so I hate you.

ROBIN

I didn't know you felt that way.

ASH

Me neither.

ROBIN

I deserve it. I guess.

ASH

No you don't.

ROBIN

No I don't.

ASH

I want to win.

ROBIN

You will.

ASH

At all of it. I want to win at all of it – the boxing, the mom thing, the dad thing.
The becoming the world champion of everything thing.
The wife thing.

ROBIN

I know.

Robin and Ash try to think of next correct thing to say.

Read: playwright not sure where to go next after two giant emotional volcanic eruption of monologuing.

Read: Playwright decides to not deal with mess she put herself + her characters in. And instead honks a Very long horn

ROBIN (cont)

HOOOOONNNNNKKK

ASH

Is that our child?

ROBIN

I should go.

ASH

Yes.

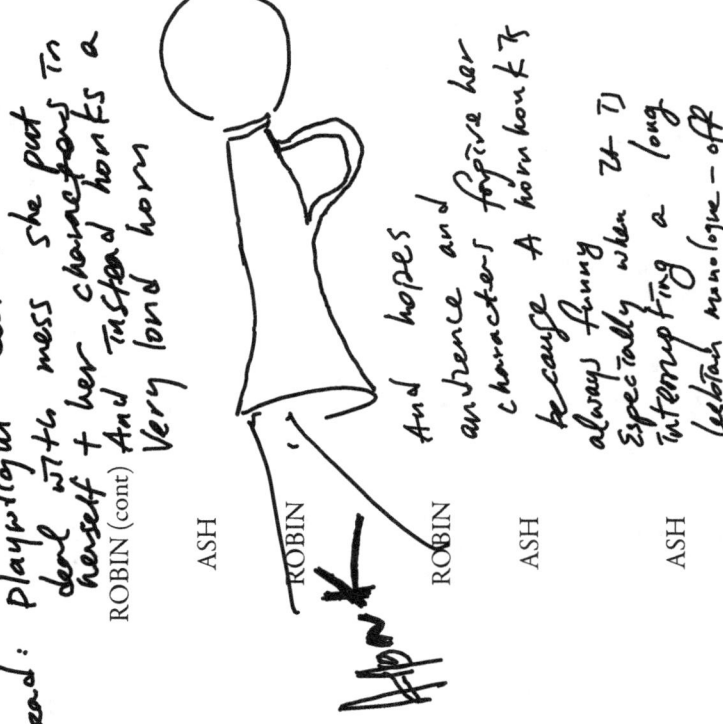

Honk

ROBIN

HOOOOONNNNNKKK

And hopes audience and characters forgive her. A horn honk is

ASH

Oh woah boy's serious.

because always funny. Especially when interrupting a long lesbian monologue-off

Jeenu I'm coming stop honking the

HOOOOONNNNNKKK

ASH

Okay I'm gonna

195

ROBIN

Go. We can talk more

ASH

later, when we get / back from

ROBIN

Yeah. Okay. Bye.

Moment of indecisive, something, do we want to, hug? Kiss?
What do you do when you're still kind of in a fight but almost resolved but your kid is bonking a horn?

Sound of car starting.

ASH

the fuck,

ROBIN

Jeenu!

They run out

ROBIN

You left the keys with / him? What is wrong with you?

ASH

I'm gonna kill him I'm gonna fucking kill him!

Offstage

ASH

Jeenu! In the passenger seat. NOW. Move over or I'm taking you to yoga.

ROBIN

Seriously? We're making yoga the punishment?

JEENU

I can't be seen with my ass in the public air.

Reluctant scuffling.

ASH

Hey, whatever works.

Car door open and shut.
Windows roll down.

ROBIN

Okay, well, I'll see you guys later.

ASH

Wanna come with?

ROBIN

For real? You won't be distracted?

ASH

Yeah, but he's pretty cute in his gear. We got some yoga-ey stuff in the club too if you still wanted

ROBIN

You sure? Ok. Ok then. Let me get my stuff.

ASH

Be quick tho I'm late!

Robin re-enters.
(*Has a moment of quiet happiness.*)
Gathers her stuff.

HONK

Coming!

ROBIN

Car rolling out driveway.

ASH
Was very much starting to lovely
for Laura Toney so many G/o want
love, actually me of a (Ariel thing want
But it's 5 years of happiness,
female of motherhood
two years of love ROBIN
Tilt Hannagan

PETER'S VOICEMAIL

(*voice of six year old boy*) This is Peter Hunt's phone. Peter is right now unavailable to pick up. Goodbye. (*inaudible sounds of a side-coaching adult*) Oh, leave a message please. Goodbye.
BEEP

RYAN

Hey, it's Ryan. Hope you got home okay the other day.
I didn't mean to chew you out like that, I just get really protective where my family is concerned.
I wanted to let you know, the boy's started at our club, it's looking good.
Uh, and if you give me your email I could send you some pictures of him in his gear.
Took some with my phone. It's cute.
He's really taking to me, and we had some cute moments.
So, don't worry so much. Kid's gonna be fine.

A boxing ring

[Go Pro]

RING ANNOUNCER (Wolf) — TIMPANI

I'm so proud to this sounds like a chamber symphony!!

Ladies and gentlemen, introducing in the red corner with black and white trunks Tommy Tavarez!
And in the blue corner, gold trunks the challenger, Ash Michaels!

RYAN — Clarinet

You nervous?

ASH — Percussion

No.

RYAN

Don't be nervous.

ASH

I'm not.

RADIO GUY (Also Wolf) — Trumpet

Ash Michaels, five foot five, hundred and forty seven pounds at 26 years old,

ROBIN *Flute*
Woohoo!!! That's my wife!!!

RADIO GUY
facing Tommy "The Tiger" Tavarez, towering over Michaels at five foot nine,

RYAN
Don't rush it, pacing!

RING ANNOUNCER
Round Number One!

DING

ROBIN
Jeenu, can you see?

WOLF *electric synths*
The wolf has a 250-degree visual range.

RYAN
Calm and steady Ash you got this

RADIO GUY

Nice left to the body by Michaels

RYAN

Good! Stay focused, three two three. Three two three.

ROBIN

Get him in the balls! Woot Woot!

RADIO GUY

Surprising speed from the rookie.

DING

RYAN

How you doing?

ASH

Good.

ROBIN

Having fun?

WOLF
The wolf will use their paws and cunning to eviscerate the prey.
GROWL

ROBIN
No no, come here. We can go say hi after fourteen more dings.

RYAN
You're doing great. Stay focused Okay?

ASH
Mmmk.

DING

RADIO GUY
Round Two!

ROBIN
Alright baby now kick some ass / kick some ass up in there!

RADIO GUY
Tavarez starts with a strong right cross,

ROBIN
WE LOVE YOU ASH MICHAELS!

WOLF
observe, calculate!

ROBIN
Jeenu, wanna cheer with? Come on, cheer with me so they can hear us.

RYAN
That's good, play it cool Ash!

ROBIN
On three, we love you Ash Michaels, ready?

WOLF
The Wolf is always ready.

ROBIN
One two three

ROBIN / WOLF
We love you Ash Michaels! We love you Ash Michaels! We love

                    RYAN / ROBIN / WOLF
                            YES!

                         RADIO GUY

Michaels scores a strong left!

                    RYAN / ROBIN / WOLF
                          Yes yes!

                         RADIO GUY

Series of blows to the body and

DING

                            RYAN
How you doing?

                            ASH
Good.

                            RYAN
Good? That was fucking excellent.

WOLF
Wolves know how to fight!

ROBIN
No no, Jeenu. Gotta wait for six more rounds

WOLF
Wolves know how to fight!

ROBIN
Okay you know what maybe we can move up.

RADIO GUY
Powerful lunge by Tavarez but the rookie steps out like ain't no thing

ROBIN
Wanna do that? Wanna find a seat in the front?

WOLF
Wolves know how to fight!

DING

ROBIN
Okay let's move closer. Come on.

DING

RYAN
Don't let him lead, don't get sucked into his pace

ROBIN
Hey Jeenu slow down wait for me.

DING

RADIO GUY
Power cross to the body! The Mexican tiger is bringing it, a narrow miss

RYAN
Slow and steady, slow-

ROBIN
Wanna cheer again?

JEENU
Yes please.

RYAN

Breathe! Three two three

ROBIN

Okay on three. One two three,

ROBIN / WOLF

We love you Ash Michaels!

RADIO GUY

Michaels backed into a corner,

ROBIN

We love you Ash Michaels!

RYAN

Keep breathing baby

RADIO GUY

The rookie takes a hook to the left.

ROBIN

No.

RYAN

Geroff the ropes get the fuck,

ROBIN

Come on Ash, we're right here, we're / all here for you okay?

RYAN

Three two three. Three two three!

DING

RYAN

Spit spit how is it how are you doing

ROBIN

They're okay, baby. It's just a game.

RYAN

(*To someone else*) Hey, Vaseline on the cut.

ROBIN

They're just playing.

DING

RYAN

Ash, Get outta there!

ROBIN

just a stupid little game

RADIO GUY

Punishing combos to the body

ROBIN

It's okay, they're gonna be just

RADIO GUY

Tiger's giving back all / he took

RYAN

Roll back!

ROBIN

No

RYAN

Move!

And another / blow to the head

RADIO GUY

RYAN / ROBIN
NO!

ROBIN / RYAN / WOLF
One Two Three

RYAN

GET UP

ROBIN / RYAN / WOLF
Four

Get up.

WOLF

ROBIN / RYAN / WOLF
Five Six

ROBIN

Stay down.

ROBIN / RYAN / WOLF
Seven Eight Nine

RYAN
Yes!

ROBIN
Shit.

RADIO GUY
Michaels is up, looks like it's a go.

RYAN
Come on Ash! Shake it off, reboot.

ROBIN
It's alright baby, You got this

RYAN
Stay up kid Few more seconds

WOLF
The hunt is impossible for the lone wolf.
You're alone in the desert, just you and your prey
Wolves suck at being alone.

Wolf escapes from Robin

ROBIN

Jeenu!

WOLF

Wolves need family.

ROBIN

Where are you going?

WOLF

There's a Korean saying, "Naturally, the arm folds inwards."

RYAN

The fuck, time out! / Stop the clock Stop the clock Hey ref!

ROBIN

Jeenu! Jeenu, Ryan / stop him

WOLF

fight for your family, back your pack, over mostly anything and anyone else.

Wolf has climbed onto the ring, Ash is distracted.

ROBIN

Jeenu.

ASH

Wha-

Bam. Ash falls
Ding ding ding.

WOLF

Howl

When a member of the pack is injured, they are groomed by the rest of the pack, for mental as well as physical support. But when the injured wolf has been separated, there is nothing to do but howl till they follow the sounds back home.

[Shift]

Wolf is asleep in Robin's lap with puppet.
Robin speaks in almost half whisper, words as lullaby.

ROBIN

And people are going crazy, leaping up, yelling Ash Michaels! Ash Michaels! I go wait in the locker rooms, as usual.
Few minutes later the Newest Amateur Golden Gloves Champion struts their butt through the door, gloves still on, smelling like a dishcloth, and they're like, undo my gloves. No kiss, not even hello, just, "undo my gloves Robs, undo my gloves"
My mind jumps, obviously, to worst possible scenario, what's wrong, what broke, on a scale of one to ten what is your level of pain – until their left hand opens up and I see, finally, the ring.
But then they are on their knee, holding up towards me the most beautiful piece of silver. And the noise melts away.
The bout, the problems with my mom, and all that is left in my head is this giant neon sign that says You keep this person.
You keep this person.
And so I did.

Robin kisses Wolf on his head.

I keep my people.

Ryan and Ash enter.

215

RYAN
C'mon Ash, that's the loss / talking, don't –

ROBIN
Guys.

ASH
Ryan, Go Home I'm tired, we can talk / some other -

ROBIN
Guys Shht!!

RYAN
What

ROBIN
He's sleeping.

RYAN
You got any beer?

ROBIN
Hushed tones, please. *(to Ash)* Honey come here, how are you?

216

ASH

I'm okay, what happened to you guys?

ROBIN

He wouldn't stop crying so I had to take him home. Are you okay? What did the doctors say?

ASH

I'm fine. It's fine. Four stitches.

RYAN

Exactly It Is Fine. It's just one bout nothing to freak out over.

ROBIN

Ry keep it down.

ASH

I'm not freaking out. I'm just saying, I just need space to think.

RYAN

About what?

ASH

About how I am going to subsist on the nothing I got for a fight I just KO'ed out on,

RYAN
You did not KO, they stopped the fight because that stupid kid hopped into the ring,

ROBIN
Okay time out, Ryan, take yourself home.

ASH
Come on Ry, we know I was losing that fight before what happened. If anything Jeenu probably saved me from getting my jaw shattered off my face.

RYAN
You don't know that. We could've turned it around -

ASH
I just need a break. For a few months maybe to figure stuff out

RYAN
What like Robin's fake maternity leave?

ROBIN
Oh, go stick your dick in a trash can.

Wolf stirs.
A moment of tension, will he wake up?

He doesn't.

ROBIN

Okay so. This boy cried for two hours before he finally fell asleep I love you both very much but if either of you wake this kid up I am going to have to kill you.

RYAN

Did you talk to him?

ROBIN

Talk to who?

RYAN

Did you get it through his head that you don't go hop into a ring when you feel like it, that you're supposed to respect other people's spaces.

ROBIN

Like how you are respecting ours?

RYAN

I'm your brother I don't have to respect my sister's space in her house.

ROBIN

Maybe your sister thinks you ought to.

RYAN Since when?

ROBIN Ryan keep your voice down.

RYAN Robin Raahhrararhaaaraahhhaararahh!

WOLF A wolf will sleep only several minutes at a time.

ASH Hey kid, how you doing? You okay?

WOLF He is always alert for lurking opponents.

ROBIN Hey sleepyhead,

RYAN Man, this kid's just got you two by your your vaginas, / he's just,

ROBIN

Ryan!

ASH

Excuse me?

WOLF

The wolf stays quiet, but hears everything,

RYAN

You wanna know why he keeps acting out? Wanna know why he fucked up your bout tonight Ash, and you know it was his fault you got nothing in your wallet right now, you wanna know why? it's coz you guys are treating him like princess fucking Disney, someone's gotta show him some discipline.

ROBIN

Who? Who's gonna do that? The high school drop out second string nothing who's living off the gym his mother bought him?

RYAN

WOLF

A wolf never attacks without learning about his prey.

ASH

He has nothing to do with this, Ry. I want to take a break for myself, okay

RYAN

Bullshit. You've got your head so far up his ass you can't even see right from wrong.

WOLF

But once the wolf attacks, it is not to wound or slow his target.

RYAN

At this point you are probably bad for the boy. Coz what's he gonna learn from you, huh?

WOLF

He attacks for one purpose only

RYAN

if it don't work out, spaz out, right?

WOLF

– to kill.

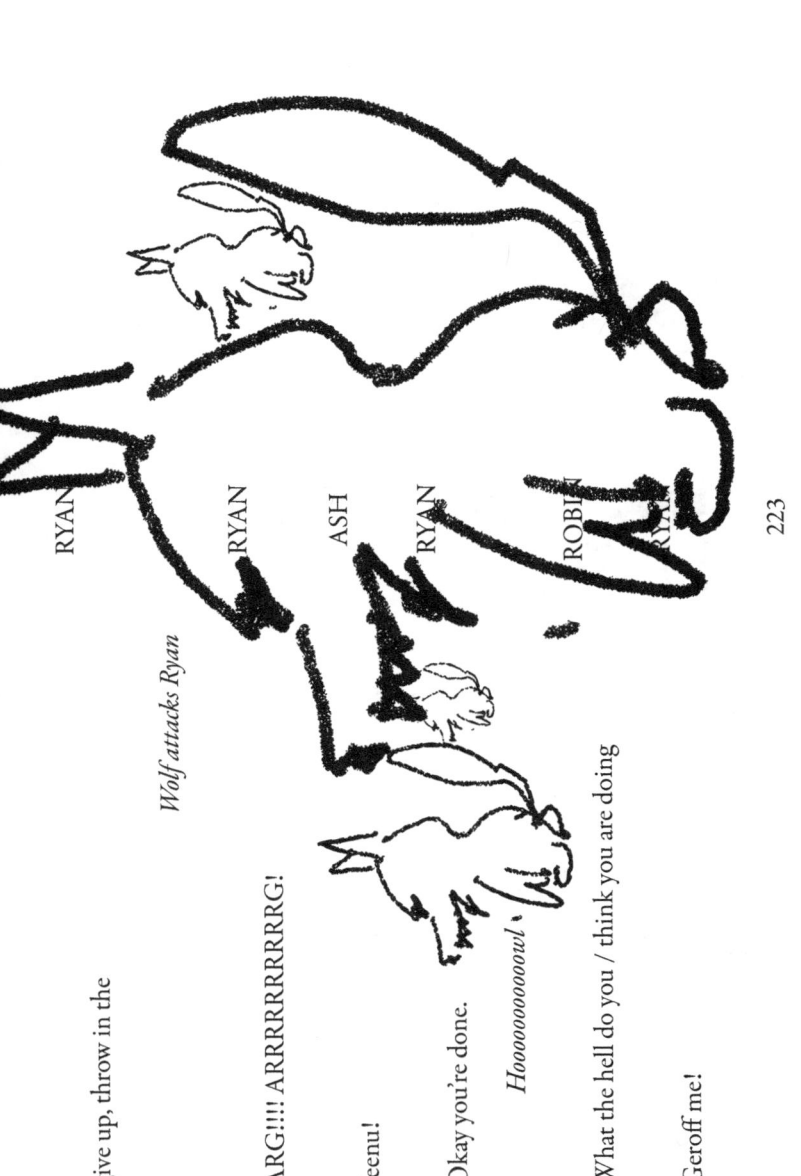

RYAN	give up, throw in the
	Wolf attacks Ryan
RYAN	ARG!!!! ARRRRRRRRG!
ASH	Jeenu!
RYAN	Okay you're done.
	Hoooooooooowl.
ROBIN	What the hell do you / think you are doing
RYAN	Geroff me!

Hoooooooooowl
Ryan takes puppet and wolf to the bathroom.
Ryan, puppet and Ash in the bathroom are depicted in shadows.

Sound of shower

RYAN

Cool down. Sit there and cool / down.

ASH

What the hell / are you doing?

Something or someone is knocked down or thrown against door etc.

RYAN

Ow! What the fuck Ash

Shower off.

ASH

Out.

No more bowl

ASH

Hey buddy, you ok? Ryan was just playing, it's okay. Come let's get you to bed, yeah? Hiho Hiho off to bed we go... No? Okay. Scooch over a bit, I'm coming in. Hey, it's so cool, you took a shower with your clothes on. Can I try?

Sound of light shower

ASH

Ah... that's so nice. It's like being in the rain. C'mere. Come. It's okay.

Ryan is back out onstage with Robin.

RYAN

(*to Robin*) It worked. I'm just saying.

ROBIN

Don't you ever dare touch that child again.

RYAN

Robs. You're overreacting.

[handwritten marginalia: "that's out of the wife's narrative / how might it be revelatory?"]

ROBIN

Ever.

RYAN

He needs discipline.

ROBIN

Not your call what he needs. No one asked you what he needs.

RYAN

I'm the only one that has the balls to be some semblance of a role model, / the fuckturd jumped into the middle of an ongoing bout,

ROBIN

You aren't his, Don't you dare call him-, Get out of my house. Get out.

RYAN

Someone's got to be the man of this family.

ROBIN

Do, whatever you need to do to get over yourself and your issues, but outside my house, away from my son. Pull some shit like that again and I promise you Ryan

RYAN

What. What will you do? You gonna choose the eBay kid over your own brother?

ROBIN

Yes. Always yes.
I choose my son. I choose my wife. Over you. Always.
Don't make me choose.

Ryan leaves.

Robin alone.
She hears, coming from the bathroom[1]:

JEENU

Does it hurt?

ASH

A little. But I'll get over it.

JEENU

Are you mad at me?

---

[1] The shadow of the puppet is now perhaps the shadow of Wolf, the actor.

227

ASH

No.
I'm just glad you didn't get hurt. Coz you could've gotten very seriously hurt. That would've made me really mad. And totally sad.

JEENU

-

ASH

Jeenu, can you promise me you won't do something like that again?

JEENU

But what if I said, I'm not what you think you see?

ASH

Hm?

JEENU

What if I said I am something else.

ASH

Like what?

JEENU

What if I said I am a wolf.

ASH

A wolf?

JEENU

Yes. And. Wolves hunt in packs. A wolf, never lets their pack's asses be whooped.

ASH

I see.
Whoever's in your pack, must feel very safe.

JEENU

It's you.

ASH

What?! It's me? I had a whole wolf in my pack? A robin and a wolf? I gotta start myself a safari!

JEENU

Robin is a robin too?

ASH

No. Robin is still human.

JEENU

But she is as pretty as a robin.

ASH

You think so?

JEENU

Sometimes. Don't tell her. Do you know how to howl? Will you howl with me?

ASH

Sure. Ready?

JEENU

Ready.

They howl.

[Daily Life 3]

Robin enters, earphones in.
Same space, different place.
She sets table for three cereals.

WOLF

Robins are a very delicate species. They don't like to fight.
They like to downward dog, and to tuck their tails under the sit bones.
They believe they can breathe through the tension. It's the truth, Robins love to breathe.

AUDIO MEDITATION (Wolf)

Take a cleansing breath in... and breathe out the tension in your body...

WOLF

See?

AUDIO MEDITATION

Feel relaxation beginning at the bottom of your feet.
It might feel like stepping into a warm / bathtub

ROBIN

MOTHERFUCKER

Robin has stepped on a lego power ranger. She pulls out her earphones and picks up enemy ranger.

ROBIN
(to lego ranger) I Hate You So Much.

Ryan enters, brushing teeth. Bacon, eggs, etc.

Ryan spits, rinses his mouth. He calls a number.

RYAN
Look, I don't know what your deal is with screening my calls, but it's not right, Ash. We should talk. Call me back.

Phone rings.

ROBIN
Hello? Mom?

Robin checks caller ID on phone. It is indeed mom.

> reminder:
> A very important formative figure for the writer

ROBIN
How, I mean, good morning to you too.

Peter enters, opens fridge and takes out a box of stale pizza.

We were just about to eat, yeah.
Cereal, probably.

Peter sprinkles some sugary cereal onto a slice of cold pizza and bites into his breakfast.

I know, I tried, but Jeenu won't eat anything else,
Oh, Jeenu is our –
oh, you know.
Of course.

Ryan calls another number

I'm glad Ryan's been keeping you in the loop. I've been so swamped with all the mom stuff,

RYAN
Robs. It's me again. You two have got to stop being dicks about this. Call me back.

ROBIN
I've been thinking about you a lot too.
A ton, actually. With Jeenu and,

Ha no. No I don't think so.
Have zero idea what I'm doing.

Really?
No of course I want to I would love that.
Let me um, get my calendar...

Robin disappears.

Wolf and puppet and Ash run in from morning run, gulps some water,

ASH
Pops or Kashi?

Puppet and Wolf point to the lucky pops.

RYAN
Mom. I've been trying you all morning.

Hope you're ok.

I'm getting worried so call me back when you get this alright?

Ryan hangs up.

ASH
You had that yesterday. And the day before. And the day before that.

Puppet and Wolf point to the grownup cereal. Reluctantly.

ASH
That's right kid. I got your number.

Ash pours the cereal, milk, hands one bowl to Wolf. They read and eat the cereal, side by side.

Peter dials a number.

Ryan gets a call.

RYAN
Hey.

PETER
Hey. What's going on.

Um.

How is he?

Peter, what are you -

I saw what happened, on the google. About the boxing game.

RYAN	PETER
	Huh?
Bout	
Bout. Nevermind. Yeah. It was pretty bad, Your kid is fine.	
	Yeah. Hey, I was wondering if, are you free? Today?
Oh. Today?	
	Or, not, or later, I'm in town so
You are?	
	Yeah. I am. It's a little, aaaag. We're separated, me and Katie – Mind if I come over? To yours?
Oh...I don't think	
	I had some ideas and I wanted to run them by you.
Um,
okay.
Yeah.
I'll text you my addy now.	

Ryan hangs up. Sends text.

ASH

What you reading today?

WOLF

There's a theory that our earth is being swallowed by water, bit by bit every day, and it is actually something we can't do much about. We can't pump the water outside of the earth, like we do when a boat is sinking, because gravity will just bring all the water back to the ground. We could evaporate them, but the sun and wind is already trying, but it ended up just bringing more water from the arctic. I think the only solution is that we could all learn how to live under water. Either we could build a billion oxygen tanks, or we could develop gills. Like how when the trees grew taller, and animals got faster monkeys stood on their feet and became humans, like that, all the mammals could become half fish. Our lungs would transform into fish lungs and we'd know how to separate the water from the air.

ASH

That's what you're reading?

WOLF

No. It is what I am thinking.

ASH

Is it for school?

WOLF

No for you. Because we are very close to the water. And I can adapt, because wolves can live in the arctic, the swamps, deserts, kitchens, and they find their way okay, but you guys are just human so I was thinking of solutions.

ASH

That's very kind and forward thinking.

I want you to like me.

WOLF

I do.

ASH

Okay.

WOLF

I like you lots.

ASH

Then why didn't you want me to come in the first place?

WOLF

Where'd you hear that?

Wolf shrugs

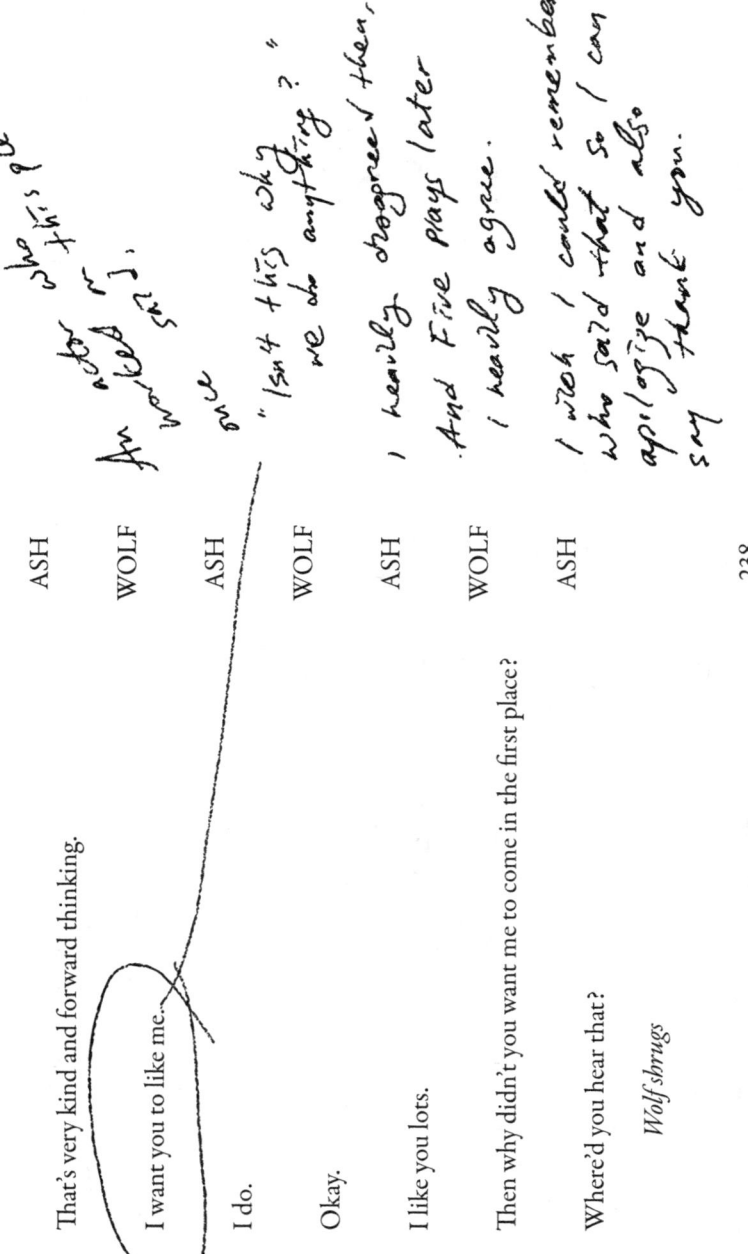

ASH An actor who's play
       worked in, said,
       once.

WOLF "Isn't this okay?
       we do anything?"

ASH   I heavily disagreed then.
      And five plays later
      I heavily agree.

WOLF

ASH   I wish I could remember
      who said that so I can
      apologize and also
      say thank you.

ASH

Esco had a tattooed hand
microphone back of their hand was
on the when for a
and I out glatfound
held the recon first pump

Been sitting on that for a while, huh?

WOLF

No.

ASH

Okay. The reason I didn't want you to come in the first place. Is because.
I didn't know you were a wolf, and
I know how hard it is for humans to deal with change and new places and new families, and I thought it was really unfair for you.
Coz it's a lot to deal with.

WOLF

(RIGHT HERE)
made true microphone fist
into the puppet "okay, fat

But I am a wolf.

ASH

Exactly. So I take it back. Cool?

WOLF

when Esco unfolded Wolf
hand into sillinan Wilkin
speak she'd bring her own
instead of fist coming from
Wolf

Okay. Do you know how to make oxygen tanks?

Robin enters

239

ROBIN
No that's not far but, or I mean if you wanted to come over. Yes here. Mom, of course you can. Any time. Any time you want. I've missed you too. Love you too. Bye.

ASH
Mom?

ROBIN
Uh huh.

ASH
Wow?

ROBIN
Uh huh.

ASH
You, okay?

ROBIN
Yeah. No. I don't know. She wants to see us.

ASH
Us? Like, us us? *(meaning Ash and Robin)*

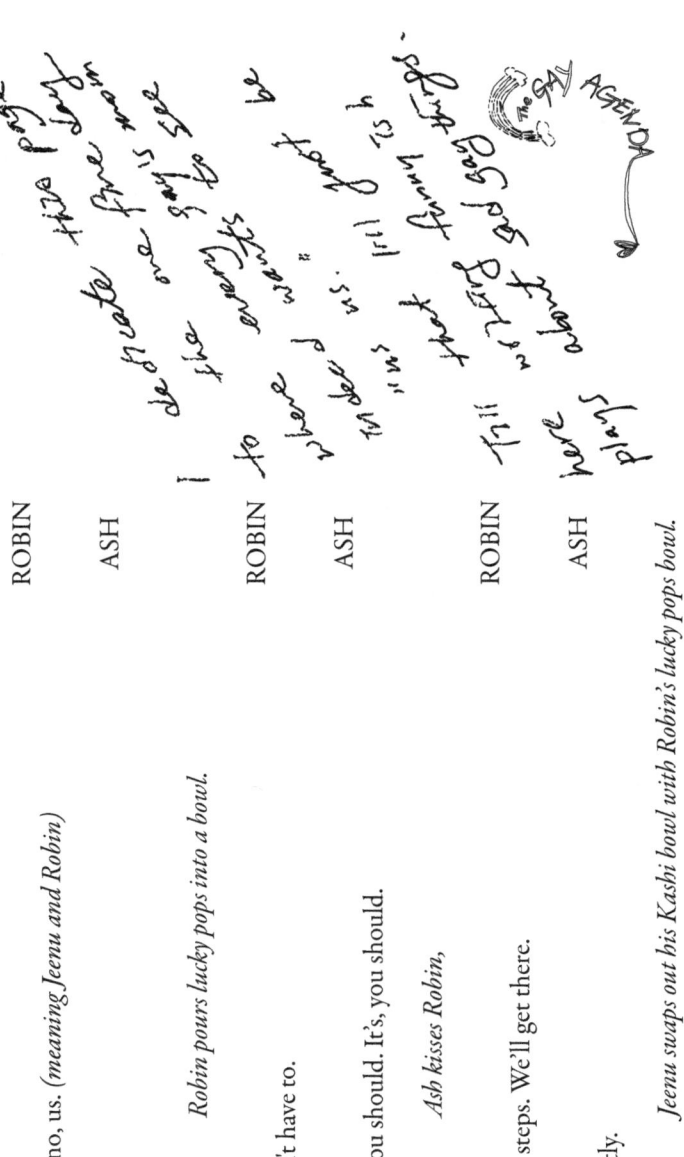

ROBIN

Um, no, us. (*meaning Jeenu and Robin*)

ASH

Oh.

Robin pours lucky pops into a bowl.

ROBIN

I don't have to.

ASH

No you should. It's, you should.

Ash kisses Robin,

ROBIN

Baby steps. We'll get there.

ASH

Exactly.

Jeenu swaps out his Kashi bowl with Robin's lucky pops bowl.

241

ASH

Jeenu.

Jeenu sadly returns lucky pop bowl to Robin.

Ding dong, someone at the door.

RYAN

Coming!

Ryan opens the door. It's Peter

PETER

I got beers. Do you do day beers?

RYAN

Come on in.

Ding! Like the end of a round of boxing.

[Knock Knock]

WOLF

Knock knock.
Say who's there.
Knock knock.

Wolf waits till audience says "Who's there"

WOLF

Donut

Wolf waits till audience says "Donut who"

WOLF

Donut do day beers with the guy who sold his kid on the internet dumbass. I can't believe you just did a knock knock joke with me. Nerds.

ROBIN (off)

Jeenu!

WOLF

Okay another one, knock knock.

Wolf waits till audience says "Who's there"

ROBIN (off)

Jeenu come here right now!

WOLF

Little Old Lady

Wolf waits till audience says "Little Old Lady who"

WOLF (cont)

Group yodel! Get it?

yodels little old lady who.

ROBIN (off)

JEEEEEEEEEEEEEEEEEENNNNNNNNNNNOOOOOOOOOOOOOOOO!

WOLF

Uh oh.

[handwritten margin notes:]
People always ask me where this came from. And sometimes also I am asked to clarify intention. And I'm like, it's called folks, it's PLAY. wait PLAY

(But I know this — I have dumped it off in a nummer of times too!) so...

[Peter and the Wolf]

Puppet on couch. Puppet playing video games.
Robin enters, with pair of small trousers.

ROBIN

Hey mister when I call you, you come to me not the other way around. Jeenu, look at me when I'm talking to you.

He does.
Robin takes a deep breath of great perseverance.
She turns the game screen off.
Robin kneels down to face the doll, eye level

ROBIN

Jeenu darling I love you you are the awesomest, can we please not put our food in our pockets.
Can we please please please never ever put spaghetti in our new, cream-colored slacks.

JEENU

Knock knock.

ROBIN

Jeenu.

Mitch had to have a piece of the puppet while we in his mouth hands used to both were playing pretend he were. I video games. I think we get bored think that more often of it was often I guess I'm a little COVID sense during the isolation but I love I can't I see we so of we so annoying

245

JEENU: Knock knock.

ROBIN: Who's there.

JEENU: Jeenu.

ROBIN: Jeenu who.

JEENU: Jee, Nu Pants are kinda hard to keep clean. (*there*)

ROBIN: Did you make that up?

Wolf and Puppet nod.

ROBIN: That's really good. I'm very proud. No more pasta in pants, okay?

Wolf and Puppet nod.

Buzzzzzz.

ROBIN

Who is it?

Game is back on.

ROBIN

Jeenu, you get five more minutes, and then piano, okay?

Robin opens door.

ROBIN

Oh. Hi.

It's Ryan.

RYAN

Hey.

> This difficult scene to really objectify Ryan only works if it comes to a head
> I think it (Ryan) behaves it feels torn begins a rear
> We can't get together sexually
> etc... begins to
> #jilbingalove

ROBIN

What do you want?

RYAN

Can I come in?

Robin lets him in.

RYAN

We need to talk. Is Ash around?

ROBIN

No.

RYAN

Where are they?

ROBIN

Out.

RYAN

They've not been to the club for a while.

ROBIN

They want a break.

RYAN

A break from what, boxing? Coz you can take a break from boxing and still pick up my calls.

ROBIN

Maybe they want a break from you.

RYAN

Family don't take breaks from each other.

ROBIN

Yes they do when family is being a dick.

RYAN

We need to talk.

ROBIN

What we've been doing.

RYAN

Drop the guard Robs. I was trying to help. I'm on your side.

— I shall let go your hand soon!

ROBIN: Who's on the other side? There is no fight. Stop trying to help.

RYAN: Peter's in town.

ROBIN: Peter who?

RYAN: His father.

ROBIN: You're joking right?

RYAN: He wants to take him back.

ROBIN: Ryan what did you do.

RYAN: Don't get all hysterical.

ROBIN

Jeenu go to your room.

RYAN

Let's be honest now you and I both know, this isn't working out.

ROBIN

Room. Now!

Wolf takes puppet to the room.

RYAN

Robs, you have got to stay calm. Peter broke off with the crazy wife, he's on his own and now he wants the kid back. He's been talking to a lawyer, okay? We thought –

ROBIN

We?

RYAN

... that it would be better to just get this cleared up before the kid gets too comfortable here.
Am I the only one who can see what's happening to this family since that kid came into this house? I barely see you any more, Ash is retiring out of the blue, you guys are just being sucked in, into this kid's Black Hole of Needs, he is breaking up our family!

RYAN

I want you to be happy. I need Ash to be happy. I know how badly you want a child and so we tried this out but Robin, it is not working. I am gonna be the bad guy and tell you the thing you are not willing to tell yourself because you are a beautiful kind stubborn-ass woman who will never give up on people. You are unequipped to take care of this child.

ROBIN

Okay.

RYAN

You have to be rational about this, think about what's best for the kid, okay?

ROBIN

Okay.

RYAN

Okay?

ROBIN

Okay.

RYAN

Good.

ROBIN
I'm gonna go help Jeenu with his piano practice, and then we're going for froyo. When we come out to go for froyo, you are not going to be here. Okay?

RYAN
Robin.

ROBIN
And you are not coming back again.

RYAN
Robin you're being

ROBIN
Mmm.
Not coming back.
Not calling.
Not anything.

RYAN
I am your brother.

ROBIN
And I love you.

When the world betrays you
And you don't know where to go.
You can always go Froyo.

253

ROBIN (cont)

And so I will forgive you. One day.
But right now, my son needs help with piano.

RYAN

He's not your son.

ROBIN

So that is where I need to be.

RYAN

The law's on his side. Pete's gonna go to court in Arizona with this if-

ROBIN

Goodbye Ry.

Robin leaves the room.
Ryan alone. And then, he leaves Robin's house.

A recorded voice rings out in the empty space.

For the 8 years
I spent writing this play
this activity was always
"math homework"
until Sarah Benson,
(a.k.a real mother
of small humans)
asked what is this
math homework
that this six year old
is doing?

JUDGE (played by wolf)

This is CV 12-1189, in the matter of Peter Hunt and Robin Shephard. Ready to proceed?

WOLF

Don't you sometimes, just wanna walk out?
or turn it off, leave the story,
You know it's not real
it's just a bunch of "what ifs"
but sometimes it feels so real

Like when the Green Ranger is under power of the evil witch and turns against the other Power Rangers, you're like that's okay don't be worried that's not actually the Green Ranger he is Jason David Frank born again Christian actor-human but still when Green Ranger defeats the Red Ranger and breaks the heart of Pink Ranger you're like nooooooooooooooooooooooooooo stop itttttt!
but then next season he comes back as the White Ranger and you're like oh phew.

Mostly, you don't walk out
you get through the moment of nooooo because you know you'll get to the phew,
but in some stories, you can't be sure
if there ever will be a phew,
in some stories, the what-ifs break away and all you get is the what-is.

WOLF (cont)

and that shit can sit in your gut like a rock for a while
And that rock is real and that rock fucking sucks
and so sometimes
you're like

what if I just walk out before it hits?
but also you're like,
what if there's a phew, coming
what if there's a phew coming that will blow that dumb rock to dust Forever
and I miss it, coz I walked out?

beat

WOLF (cont)

You ready to do this?
Let's do this!

[**pull**]

A boxing ring, four adults, four corners.

JUDGE[2]

This is CV 12-1189, in the matter of Peter Hunt and Robin Shephard.

WOLF

You wanna do this? Let's do this.
Ladies and gentlemen, introducing in the right corner, the challengers Team Hunt
And in the left corner, the world champions of everything, Team Shephard-Michaels!

Everyone raises their right hand.

JUDGE

Do you swear the testimony you are about to give is the whole truth and nothing but the truth so help you God?

ALL

I do.

WOLF

Round number one!

DING

---

[2] Judge's voice is a recorded voice, a new voice we have never heard before.

257

ROBIN
Presenting the documents related to original power of attorney signed and dated,

PETER
The fact is, a Power of Attorney document does not transfer custody permanently

ROBIN
The affidavit of waiver of interest in child is permanent

PETER
We approached the defendants with desire to nullify contract, induced fraudulently

ROBIN
Your honor, there was absolutely no direct contact with Mr. Hunt since the initial hand off

DING

WOLF
Robins are a very delicate species. They don't like to fight. But sometimes a downward dog can turn into a bite because wolves fight for each other.

PETER
Petitioner would like to call to the stand, Mr. Ryan Shephard

WOLF

But the omega wolves like dumbass Ryan -

RYAN

Yeah I was there, he thought I was Ash. But on the other hand, we thought the kid was like two years old so -

DING

PETER

Claim of information fraud has been corroborated

WOLF

Peters love papers, a fortress of papers

ROBIN

the real question is why it's okay to put your child up on the internet

PETER

the real question is why it's okay to lie about being a dyke

ROBIN

Objection, argumentative

WOLF

We love you Robin Shephard! We love you -

PETER

Respondent's domestic partner displayed acts of violence toward the petitioner

WOLF

Wolves can't let their pack's asses be whupped

DING

DING

RYAN

Yeah, Ash punched the guy, and yes it was uncalled for, but honestly he was asking for it

ASH

What does that have anything to do with

WOLF

Wolves know how to fight!

ROBIN

Your honor, this is irrelevant information regarding the issue at hand.

PETER

It's evidence that the child was placed in a hostile environment

WOLF

Peters worry too much, Wolves can adapt, to anywhere

PETER

Ms. Ashley Michaels to the stand

WOLF

Right foot forward

ASH

I was late that day, yes, when Jeenu was dropped off at our house,

WOLF

Guard up, like Hello.

ASH

No, it was not because we were trying to hide we were fucking married.

WOLF

We love you Ash Michaels!

ASH
They put a child on the internet. Would You agree to get a kid from the internet?

WOLF
Yes!

PETER
Did you or did you not want him there on that day, answer the question.

ASH
No I did not want a child I do not know being dropped off at my house, like a book I got off of Amazon.

WOLF
What?

PETER
No further questions.

ASH
Who does that?

PETER
Thank you, Ms. Michaels.

                    DING

                                        WOLF
                                        Um, something about, oxygen tanks,

                    DING

PETER
The documents are based / on the date of agreement

ASH
What about the affidavit!

                    DING

                                        WOLF
                                        gills, under water, to separate the, um,

                    DING

ROBIN
Under the Federal laws, state laws forbidding / joint adoption by same-sex couples is illegal

PETER

Temporary Custody

ROBIN / ASH

Designed to be irrevocable!

DING

WOLF

DING

the trees grew taller, and animals, to separate the, um, monkeys from humans, no, water from the,

RYAN

Hostile / environment for the

ROBIN

Durable Power / of Attorney contract withstands

PETER

Temporary custody, / as are the limits of

ASH

Who does that?

DING

WOLF

I'm a wolf. I am a lone wolf. I have to

DING

PETER

The doctor mints are based on the date of a green mint [the documents are based on the date of agreement]

ASH

What about the **after David!** [affadavit]

WOLF

What's an after david?

ROBIN

Under Fred's evil claws, the claws / for bleeding joint abortion by same-saying couplets isn't evil [Under the Federal laws, state laws forbidding joint adoption by same-sex couples is illegal]

PETER

Temper / baby cuts the meat! [Temporary Custody]

ASH

Designed /to be a record table! [irrevocable]

265

ROBIN: **Gerbil power / of a bunny** [Durable power of attorney]

PETER: for **temper baby cuts the meat!** [Temporary Custody]

ROBIN / ASH: Look at the **After David** [affadavit]

DING

WOLF: Excuse me, what is the / After David?!

DING

RYAN / PETER: Power of a **bunny is temper baby** [attorney is temporary]

DING

WOLF: Anyone?

Really had the best time coming up with these words with nonsense

CHRIS BANNON
JIN HA
ESLO JONLEY
NICOLE VILLAMIL
IAN QUINLAN
DUSTEN WILLS

Thank you for your IMPACT.

DING

ROBIN

It's stunning that this **prepped kiss of never riding children on the internet, does not seem to violin hate** any [practice of advertising children, does not seem to violate]

WOLF

What are you saying?

ROBIN

Presenting **After David of Razor** of Interest in Child [Affidavit of waiver]

ASH

Who does that?

ROBIN

A Record Table after the 11th day it was motorized [Irrevocable after the 11th day it was notarized]

ASH

But for the child's sake,

PETER

To come to an agreement

ROBIN

No.

ASH

To settle

RYAN

for the child's sake

ROBIN

Jeenu's interests are

PETER

What's better for the boy.

a breath

JUDGE

I understand there was a motion to interview the child in chambers.
If there's no other evidence or testimony to be presented, we'll call the child forth to put on tape

ASH

Jeenu?

PETER

Junior?

RYAN

Well, say something.

Everyone looks at puppet

JEENU

...

WOLF

I don't want to do this any more.

Wolf leaves the puppet, and walks out of the story.

[Daily Life 4]

Same Space, trying to be a different space,

Puppet sits alone, sans Wolf.

Ryan brushing teeth. Phone rings.

Peter opens fridge and takes out a box of stale Pizza, also on phone.

ASH
Morning champ.

RYAN
Hi mom.

PETER
No I didn't get custody.

Robin watches these people go about their performances, not sure what next to do.

ASH
How'd you sleep?

RYAN
Depends on when they set the court date, I don't know.

PETER
They didn't get him either.

PETER

I told you, the State has him. I don't know why Katie!

ASH

Wanna go for a run?

RYAN

They're fine.

Because we fucked up!

Let's go for a run. / Just a quick one before-

He's / fine.

Because you put our son on / the internet Katie.

It's just temporary! I didn't! The guy showed up / at my door, it wasn't me, okay?

Yep, you're right about that he's not our son

Or, cereal?

You made sure of that.

Pops or Kashi?

Robin disappears the stage space (lights, curtains, whatever you got)

It's just Robin and her son.
Robin holds the lifeless puppet, sets him, touches his arms, face, little legs... tries to connect to the Wolf through the object,

and then an idea:

ROBIN

What if I said
I am not what you think you see.
I am not human, this floor is forest earth, and to the left of that glaring exit light, a river flows,
You are not what you feel you are, you are a spider, an eagle
Or a wolf.
What if I said you are a wolf?
What if I said you are the single most important breath in my space. You are the first gear that turns the clock of my world.
What if I said I will fight for you with every blood cell and cranial nerve I possess.

A tiny entrance.
Wolf returns, like a little childhood memory.
Robin addresses Wolf.

ROBIN

And you believed me?
Does that change anything?

End of Play

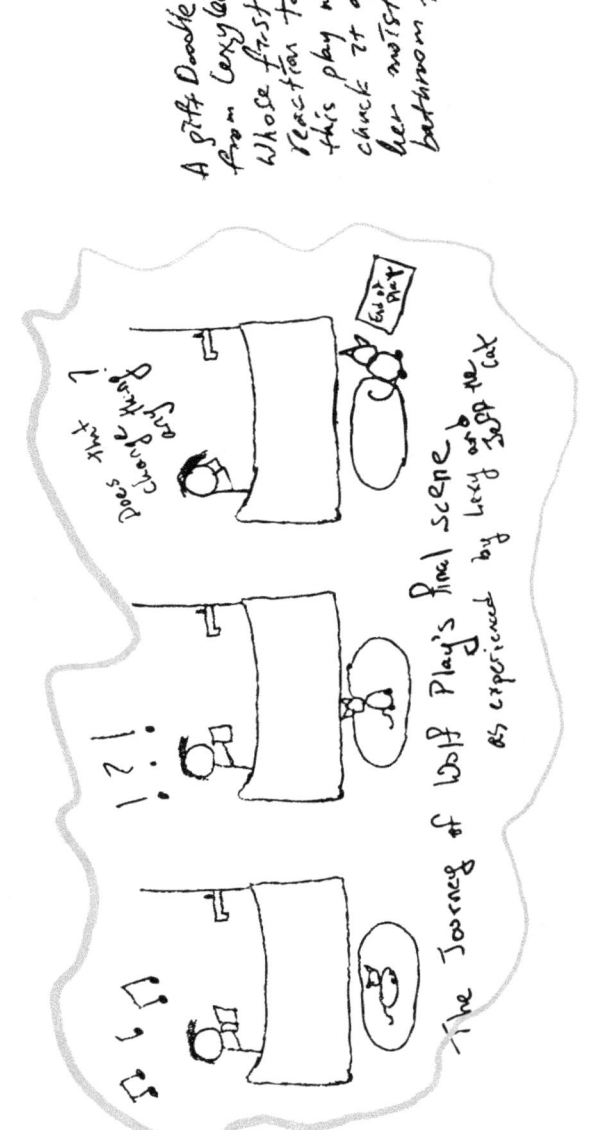

No More Sad Things

— Gift Doodle from Jules Ockey who gifted me a most beautiful first professional world premiere ever and the 7 years later moved to Australia and broke my heart... ♡

CHARACTERS

JESSIEE   Female, thirty-two years old. Any ethnicity.
KAHEKILI   Male, fifteen years old. Hawaiian.
GUIDEBOOK   A guide through things. Any ethnicity.

SETTING

Maui, Ka'anapali Beach

TIME

Now

AUTHOR'S NOTES

–   a cut-off either by self or other.
,   at end of a line marks an interruption of thought by another character, not necessarily a line cut-off.
/   a point where another character might cut in.
[words] that aren't spoken in words

Original songs by Hansol Jung and Jongbin Jung.

It would be nice if Guidebook plays Polynesian drums and ukulele, and has a lovely voice.

TRANSLATIONS
huhu: angry
honu: turtle
haole: foreigner
lolo: crazy
ule: penis
chiho: expression of total excitement
kahuna: priest, sorcerer
hele mai: come here

A boy with an ukulele.
He is a metaphorical guidebook.

A hello.

He sings

GUIDEBOOK

(sings)	(translation)
He nani lua ʻole	*Of unsurpassed beauty*
Kuʻu wehi o nā lani	*Is my heavenly adornment*
He kilohana ʻoe	*You are a finely crafted kilohana*
Naʻu e pūlama mau	*That I shall always cherish*
Hōʻolu i ka poli e	*Comforting my heart*
Mehana i ke anu e.	*Bringing warmth to the cold*
Mau loa ke aloha	*Love is everlasting*
i kō puʻuwai hāmama	*Because of your generous heart*
He uʻi lani ʻoe	*You are a heavenly beauty*
Naʻu e mālama mau	*For me to always treasure*
Aia i ka laʻi e	*Existing in tranquility*
Hemolele i ka mālie.	*Flawless there in the calm*

This is a song.
Malie's Song, or the Hawaiian Lullaby.
This is an instrument.
Ukulele, or Hawaiian interpretation of the Portugese cavaquinho.
This is a stage.
Theatrical Space, or our collective deep dark weird dreams.

Song ends.

Welcome

[handwritten note: I recited this version for he has since agreed to be in WOLF PLAY.]

[handwritten note: This page is dedicated to my work husband BRIAN QUIJADA who I met on this play. He has since refused to be in any of my other plays what a dick]

[handwritten: → Jordans.]

JESSIEE

I have a dream.
Frogs. Thousands of them all over the house,
croaking jumping laying eggs in the kitchen sink.
I'm terrified I hate frogs who doesn't hate frogs
So I call the frog killing people –
hello please I have frogs I want them gone
and they come in with these huge pliers
I'm talking massive six-foot-tall men with six-foot-tall pliers
they start snipping away at the frogs, snip, snip, snip,
with the control of Mister Miyagi from *Karate Kid*,
you know, shnip,
hai, super chopsticks!
then back to noodles.

Hours and hours they snip away at my house
and then finally they shake my hand and announce:

GUIDEBOOK
"Congratulations, your house is sterile, we will now take our pay."

JESSIEE
In a flash the pliers turn into giant forks and they fork away all of my
furniture. All of it, the table, the bed, the little Russian dolls with
toothpicks in their heads – So I'm left in this sterile house, with
Nothing left in it, the walls are barely standing.
Then I hear, this little,

GUIDEBOOK
Ribbit. Ribbit.

JESSIEE
I follow the sound,

 GUIDEBOOK
Ribbit ribbit.

JESSIEE
It's coming from inside my bathroom.
I'm like, ho, got you now sucker.
Bam, swing open the door and yah! Sure enough

GUIDEBOOK
Ribbit ribbit ribbit ribbit.

JESSIEE

There he is, a little tadpole stuck to the wall of my toilet bowl.
Our eyes meet.
No one breathes.
Then he grows legs and arms and he's a friggin' frog in two seconds!
I get an urge, a massive six-foot-tall plier urge to squash it,
but when I reach out my hands the little thing starts singing.
Yah, singing! In perfect John Denveresque croony tenor he goes,

GUIDEBOOK

Let me know your eyes, warm as the sun
mold your secrets, deep as your heart
trace your lips, till night turns to morning
Don't need a lot
Let me be part of your body

JESSIEE

– jumps on to my index finger – the one that was about to squash him –
and the little thing chirps in his little frog voice,

GUIDEBOOK

"Bye Mommy,
I'm not mad you had to kill me.
Come find me in Maui."

KAHEKILI

I have dis dream,
eva since I can remember.
Dis lady, yah, sitting on da shore.
She lift up her eyes, an' stay on my eyes, li'dat a long long time
like she t'ink I know her, like she want that I know her
But I'm jus',
I don't.
I want fo' say sumt'ing, "Hello, who are you, can I help you?"
But I open my mout', an' not'ing come out.
Usually, y'know, I got dis loud talk nobody not hear my talk,
my fadda say all da time –

GUIDEBOOK

"Kahekili, you wen gone swallowed da thunder, boy,
when you gon' / learn fo' whisper like da kine normal people?"

KAHEKILI

Learn fo' whisper like da kine normal people yadda yadda ya...
But in dis dream, no way dis mout' gon' sound.
Den dis lady she get angry or jus' bored I don know,

KAHEKILI (cont)
but she leave my eyes, walk into da watah an' tek off,
An' I stand stuck in da sand,
li'dat stuck in da sand wid dis stupid silent mout',
jus' watchin' dis lady's head up an' down up an' down,
jus' watchin' da waves, da breaks, eat her up
Dass when I hear it.
Dis voice, song, sumt'ing, I hear it go,

GUIDEBOOK

"Psst. Psst psst."

KAHEKILI

I look around, li'dat, li'dat,
den da sound again,

GUIDEBOOK

"Psst psst. Psst psst."

KAHEKILI

I'm still like, huh?
An' den da buggah go,

GUIDEBOOK

"Psst. Kahekili."

KAHEKILI
I look up, an' up deh da most biggest star, neh,
she blink blink psst psst gon' crazy li'dat.
Dis my dream, y'know so I can da kine, fly,
I fly fly fly not like da Superman but like da watahman on da breaks,
fly fly fly.
Den just when I get up deh, close enough fo' some talk
dis buggah sings.
Outta da blue li'dat da buggah sings,

GUIDEBOOK
Let me know your fingers, soft as the sun
mold your fists, big as your heart
trace your arms, till night turns to morning
Don't need the stars
Let me be part of your body

KAHEKILI
Den she kiss me on da fron' a da head,
turn my body into one star, li'dat everyt'ing jus' hard rock hard.

KAHEKILI (cont)
An' befo' I can say stop I'm da star and she not,
she fall an' fall an' fall toward da watah,
but I can hear her she call out fo' me, she go she go,

GUIDEBOOK
"Bye baby, I'm not sad you never knew me
I'll find you in Maui."

(as guidebook)
The best and only way to get to Maui is air travel. Although Hawaii's islands lie in close proximity to each other, the currents of the Pacific run so deep and wild through the channels, that not even the bravest of sea warriors could brave the waves.
But while you're up there, be sure to peer down at the great island of paradise. The shape of Maui has been likened to that of a snowman, lying diagonally towards west, embracing all weary travelers from near and far.

JESSIEE
Hate planes. Hate, hate, hate planes.
I'm sitting in 25A, squashed up between a view of the Pacific sea,
and this very huge marine and his tales of nine different spinal surgeries.
Two hours in and he's about to show me a scar that –

GUIDEBOOK
"Runs from my ear to the shoulder blade, blade to the T12, T12 to bladder,
then to the tailbone. Kinda looks like a dragon. A skinny dragon."

JESSIEE
So I pretend to fall asleep.
Which he takes as a cue to fall asleep too.
On my shoulder.
I'm thirty-two – too old for this to be cute, you know?
But I'm stuck here, barely breathing for the fear of cracking yet another
thoracic something in this poor man's body.
And I could just hear my mom,

GUIDEBOOK
"Ha, think you can leave me here and be free,
that's where you end up, wedged in there like a thumb in an asshole."

JESSIEE
No, that's unfair. She'd never say that.
In fact, she's barely said anything in the past couple months.
She's depressed. She's –
But no more sad things.

MAUI ^^

JESSIEE (cont)

My mom, bless her soul,
is the most angelic, beautiful, clueless person in the world,
faithful to the church, faithful to the world, faithful to her faith.
She got cancer somewhere in the knees, had to get them both chopped off,
the cancer and the knees – not that it helped – still thinks the worst thing
about being legless is that she can't kneel down to pray.
So when I announced that I'm,
headed for the hulas and Mai Tais of the west sun,
all she said was,

GUIDEBOOK

"Be safe, okay?"

JESSIEE

I said I'd bring back a grandchild for her,
would she mind boy or girl or something in between.
She said,

GUIDEBOOK

"Oh, oh, how about those, macadamia nut things covered with chocolate?
Those are Hawaiian, aren't they?"

JESSIEE

I'm thinking serves me right,
abandoning your legless mom to go catch a frog,
I'm thinking, yeh, this right here is the rest of the trip,
my smallness wedged between the world's rude largeness,
no way I'll ever budge from my small stupid seat.
And then I start to feel funny, count the dates and realize,
Yay, menstruating.
To my right, dreaming marine, to my left, the Pacific.
What to do?
Stay put and soon we'd both be sitting in a pool of blood
– day one, I go pretty anemic –
Climb out from my gorge, and I might break him or wake him
and well
he looked so peaceful.
So what's a girl to do?
This is what I do.
Find a tampon, slide hand into pants – all of which are expertly concealed
by coat and blanket. Then slowly, silently, with the focus of Mister Miyagi,
Pop the sucker in. Yup, all this in the confines of 25A, y'all.
The audacity of taking care of personal needs in public spaces.
That's accomplishment, people.
And I was like, yeh. I can do this, I'm going to Maui.

KAHEKILI

Love planes. Love, love, love planes.
Bruh, what miracle, y'know, flyin'.
Monster engine growl down da road,
den wind an' air tek over, li'dat, tek over,
lift up dis whole mansion a people up, up, up, an'
whooooooooshshhhhmmm.
Was one trip wid my fadda, y'know, dis plane ride.
Dis boy, ten years old, fadda an' son, we's goin' pipeline.
Billabong Pipeline Masters, dass one odda Triple Crown of Surfing, y'know.
Shoots, bruh, dis my fadda's time, any one back home dey know,
Haw, he can ride any kine wave, dis kine dat kine all da kines,
he be taking one odda t'ree triple crowns, fo' sure
Nanahnanahnanahnanah!

he neva got it.
We neva even got deh. Pipeline beach? Nah.
He took wid us his woman, yah?
dey fight every minute an' second,
an' li'dat all *huhu* she leaves us
da night befo' da fuckin' day of the tournament,
an' he go drunk walk all over Waikiki till
some tourist wen run over his big toe.
You wanna kill da rising surfer, plenny easy. Jus' buss up da buggah's big toe.
Fadda neva say any kine t'ing about dat accident.
Neva say any kine t'ing about anyt'ing no more,
jus' sit deh carving tiny *honu* from scraps a wood, eh,
honu keyring, *honu* magnet *honu* whatevadafuck,
fucking ugly little buggahs.
Sell 'em on da beach fo' da *haoles*, da kine tourist.
Dat plane back home. Dat be my second an' last plane ride.
To my right, tiny window.
To my left, tiny man.
My shrinking fadda wid da drinks, wid da cryin'.
Dis boy, dis ten-year-old boy doing any t'ing he can
to not stare at dis fadda's buss up toe,
to not stare at dis hero giant, da kine, neh.
An' I remember t'inking, Today one life wen pau.
Dis buss up toe, it wen *pau* one life.
Dat life not my life.
My life neva gon' drink one drink,
neva gon' go *lolo* ova li'dat, a woman.
No need fly anyweh other place,
No need no odda person,
Me I'm gon' keep all a my toes stayin' right here, in my island, Maui.

284

In-flight seat belt release: "ping"

GUIDEBOOK
Aloha and welcome to Maui Hawaii, one of the most desired destinations on the planet. With over two and half million visitors almost every year, we know that you know that Maui is the most happiest place to be.

KAHEKILI
Marry me.

GUIDEBOOK
[Ukulele strum] !!

JESSIEE
We should tell the stories in order.

KAHEKILI
Marry me.

GUIDEBOOK
[Ukulele strum] ...

JESSIEE
People will be confused.

KAHEKILI
Marry me! Jessiee with two ees. Marry me.

GUIDEBOOK
[Ukulele strum]?
[Ukulele strum] ...?

JESSIEE
So he asks me, out of the blue to marry him.
I've known this guy for what, barely a week, so I say...

This isn't working.

JESSIEE (cont)
This isn't working. Start at the beginning.

GUIDEBOOK
[Ukulele strum] ... :(

JESSIEE

I said, back it up!

GUIDEBOOK

With over two and half million visitors almost every year, we know that you know that Maui is the most happiest place to be.

In-flight seat belt release: "ping"

GUIDEBOOK

(as flight captain) Aloha and welcome to Maui, the current temperature is 79 degrees, local time is Friday, January 26, 2:52 a.m. Thank you for flying with us this morning, we hope you enjoy your stay. Mahalo.

JESSIEE

With a thud, the plane lands,
I bid good luck to Mister Marine,
watch him hug the life out of some sleepy happy girl.
The whole airport smells of sleepy happy people. I'm a bit lost.
I've never done this before you know, travel for pleasure.
I consult the guidebook and he says,

GUIDEBOOK

Ka'anapali Ka'anapali
Pretty Paradise at sea
Ka'anapali

KAHEKILI

Ka'anapali Beach.
Usually not good for mornings, too small an' lappish da surf stay yeh?
We watahmen call dose tourist waves,
good for pictures good for paddling good for not'ing.
But today, I t'ink,

GUIDEBOOK

Ka'anapali

KAHEKILI

I wek up look up at da sky an' t'ink,

GUIDEBOOK

Ka'anapali

JESSIEE

So I think okay, why not.

GUIDEBOOK
Where the waves are young and free
Ka'anapali

GUIDEBOOK *(As rental car receptionist)*
Yeah, man, we're all out of the open cars, they go pretty fast, you know?
All we got is a couple compacts and a whole lotta SUVs.
Do you want insurance with that?

Jessiee's phone rings. She ignores it.

GUIDEBOOK *(still rental car guy)*
Blue Hyundai straight down, somewhere on your left.
Have fun, man, *mahalo*.

Grab a board and ride the passing tide
Grab a snorkel let the worries slide
Everything's easy, in Ka'anapali

When the coral reefs come out to play
Ocean wonders brighten up the bay
Of Ka'anapali

JESSIEE & KAHEKILI
Ka'anapali.

KAHEKILI
Strange how quiet it stay dis day.
Even early morning y'know, eh, people laughin', gettin' drunk somewhere.
Ka'anapali stay separate planet on Maui – Planet Tourist.
But dis day not one buggah, not one sound.

JESSIEE
The whole place is lit by the stars.
I've never seen anything lit by the stars before.

KAHEKILI
Den deh by da shore I see da lady y'know, from my dream,

Jessiee's phone rings.

KAHEKILI (cont)
And I thought, lady has phone, kay, not my dream.

A loud splash, a body thrown into a mass of water. No more phone.

KAHEKILI
First t'ought, fucking tourists fucking stop chucking shit into my *'aina* –
Second t'ought, lady jus' t'row her phone in da sea.
Normal people don't do dat.

GUIDEBOOK
Off of the point, there are strong currents at times, so use caution.

KAHEKILI
Aloha, howzit, eh?

JESSIEE
My god, you scared me!

KAHEKILI
Haw, sorry, jus', everyt'ing good? You good, eh?

JESSIEE
Excuse me?

KAHEKILI
You t'rew your phone into da watah.

JESSIEE
Oh. Yes. I did.

KAHEKILI
Y'know I don't know how come you do dat but you shouldn't do dat. Maybe you wen hit swimming *honu* on his head an' den his 300-year-old life *pau*.

JESSIEE
Excuse me?

KAHEKILI
Have to stay respectful odda ocean, y'know.

JESSIEE
Sorry. You're probably thinking, stupid tourists,

KAHEKILI
Fo' sure, but you t'inking, stupid locals, so we even, neh? So how come you do dat?

JESSIEE
Do what? Oh, phone. I'm, getting off the grid.

JESSIEE (cont)
You know, Maui, no worries, free as a bird,

KAHEKILI
Maui is off da grid, yah?

JESSIEE
If you're from Akron, Ohio, yeah.

KAHEKILI
Kay den, how come you getting off da grid?

JESSIEE
Funny story actually – Do you want the bullshit version or the real one.

KAHEKILI
Da funny one.

JESSIEE
Maybe it's not that funny. I'm visiting, taking a well-deserved break from my busy important life -

KAHEKILI
Yah, dass not dat funny.

JESSIEE
Actually I'm an escaped convict
running from the international police
with my bag full of cash and high- grade dope.

KAHEKILI
Haw.

JESSIEE
Yup.

KAHEKILI
Fo' real?

JESSIEE
Yeah, for real. Wanna look? Look.

Jessiee holds out her bag.
Kahekili takes a look, tentative.

JESSIEE (cont)
Ohmygod you totally / fell for that!

KAHEKILI
Yah yah well you gon' say sumt'ing about money and dope most Hawaiian boys gon' wan' look.

JESSIEE
Sorry to disappoint I'm just a little ol' girl with her boring little knapsack looking for her long-lost chance at happiness.

KAHEKILI
Ah, you one a dose.

JESSIEE
One of what?

KAHEKILI
Plenny mainland people come Maui fo' find "happiness."

JESSIEE
Glad to be clumped in with the general public.

KAHEKILI
You angry! I apologize,
I only say you come da right place.

JESSIEE
Not angry at all. I'm generally clumped in with the general public. I spring from the heart of that general indistinguishable lump of boring, small and predictable.

KAHEKILI
I only meant you have come to da right place.

JESSIEE
Thanks, I guess.
...
I don't normally do this.

KAHEKILI
?

JESSIEE
This, with you, I don't like talking to strangers,

                KAHEKILI
        "My name is Kahekili Ke'aloha. Nice to meet you."
        Now we good.

                JESSIEE
        Totally. All better.

                KAHEKILI
        "And what is your name, miss?"

                JESSIEE
        Nicole.

                KAHEKILI
        Nicole...

                JESSIEE
        Kidman.

                KAHEKILI
        Like da movie actress, neh?

                JESSIEE
        It's a joke.

                KAHEKILI
        You a funny lady.

                JESSIEE
        Not really.

                KAHEKILI
        Kay den, "Ms. Kidman, the surfs are most beautiful
        today. Might I interest you to be scuba diving for
        happiness?"

                JESSIEE
        He's quick funny and hot as a nugget.
        I see his hands roughed up by waves and sands I imagine,
        his dark black hair, wetted to his tanned forehead, glimmering on
        a sunny...
        I am very much sexing out on this surfer man.

                KAHEKILI
        Y'know, Ka'anapali Beach is da most popular beach for
        safe scuba diving.

[handwritten margin notes:] This is such a terrible joke people always laughed / So I kept it... but still unsure why people laughed at / Because so dumb that it's actually funny? / LARA MERCADO this character you written has all over her...

JESSIEE
You know how exotic vacation spots do that to you.
It's like a little travel package: tiny toiletries, large libido.

KAHEKILI
Or maybe surfing?
Great breaks today for first time surfers.

JESSIEE
He keeps talking and talking and I keep dreaming the wrong...

KAHEKILI
You not know happiness till you wen meet dis
'aina's rippling waves, li'dat.

JESSIEE
And I'm like, Ripple me home honey.

KAHEKILI
We go neh?

JESSIEE
Uh, I'll think about you, it.

KAHEKILI
Dass one no, I know, when lady say, I'll t'ink about it,
it means take a walk, fella.

JESSIEE
Yup, that's a no.

KAHEKILI
How come?

JESSIEE
Can't swim.

KAHEKILI
Wha!

JESSIEE
What.

KAHEKILI
I don't know what dat's like. Can't swim.

JESSIEE
It's not a disability or anything I just don't do it,

KAHEKILI
I teach you, eh? All da time I do dis.

JESSIEE
Do what, seduce unassuming ladies into
waddling into the water with you and then
have your way with them?
Coz I'm not against that.

KAHEKILI
I just meant swimming, eh, but if you go li'dat,
y'know. I'm not against.

JESSIEE
If you're not and I'm not, ...why are we...not?
And I'm thinking, where did that come from?

KAHEKILI
You a funny lady.

JESSIEE
Funny ladies are softer on the inside.
Wanna find out?
Seriously, who's this woman talking?

KAHEKILI
She mek me laugh, like a long time ago.

JESSIEE
And maybe the sand on my bare feet is just foreign enough.

KAHEKILI
And maybe da breaks odda beach, rhythm enough.

JESSIEE
Maybe his fingers, familiar enough.

KAHEKILI
Maybe her laugh, sad enough.

They kiss long enough, sweet enough.

JESSIEE
Read somewhere, we keep our trauma locked up in our muscles,

KAHEKILI
Someone say, we keep our stories hidden in da body,
can not shake it off, can not let it go,

JESSIEE
And sometimes, we find someone that finds them. Our hidden stories.

They think.
Then they do it again, longer, warmer.

KAHEKILI
I'm on plane, flying again, Monster engine between my thighs,

JESSIEE
Like the ocean, He moved like the ocean.

KAHEKILI
Whoooooooshshshmmmm. An' den we lift up, up, up.

JESSIEE
And I'm thinking
"What are you doing, Jessiee. Step on the brakes, Jessiee.
Also, if you're gonna do this, chuck your tampon Jessiee.

KAHEKILI
Wha?

JESSIEE
Hmm?

KAHEKILI
You t'rew somet'ing over,

JESSIEE
What?

KAHEKILI
I t'ink I saw – You t'rew something into da sea.

JESSIEE
Glass, pebble, thing, it was, you know, my back,
something hurting my back, or tampon, it was my
tampon, I threw my tampon into your sea.

KAHEKILI
Haw.

JESSIEE
It is biodegradable.

KAHEKILI
Wha?

JESSIEE
Dissolves. Into fish food.

KAHEKILI
Haw.

JESSIEE
Should I go get it back?

KAHEKILI
Nah.

JESSIEE
That's worse, right?

KAHEKILI
Yah.

{ Hehehe }

Guidebook expertly intervenes,
with very beautiful ukulele sounds ... :)

JESSIEE
Our clothes lay on the shore,

KAHEKILI
          Our bodies wrapped widda sand,

JESSIEE
The stars were unbelievably, many.
And then something strange happens,
maybe he did hit a memory nerve.
Somewhere between his ribs and my belly, a slide of his palm
and I am back   een years, high school,
with a voice of a boy I'd long locked away.

BOY *(Played by* GUIDEBOOK.*)*
So that one's Ursa Major, you know the Big Dipper, right?
And that's her son, Ursa Minor. Ursa is Latin for bear.

JESSIEE
A boy obsessed with constellations,
poking holes into his milk box sky for the science fair.

BOY
These four outline the body, the ladle part is the tail.

JESSIEE
He was going through all of the holes he had poked,
going through all of the stories behind those holes.
Love of my life, today his best friend was the toothpick.

BOY
Then one day, the boy hunter was roaming the woods,
as was the lady bear. In one sad fated moment, the two locked
eyes, Callisto in bear form, rushed towards the boy hunter,
to give him a hug, or to beat the shit out of him, I don't know,
but the boy hunter thought the latter, coz he

BOY & JESSIEE
Got out his bow and arrow, swift as lightning, drew the sinew,

BOY
And just before something really sad happened,

BOY & JESSIEE
A divine intervention.

JESSIEE
Story goes, Zeus, who'd originally knocked up Callisto, felt bad and so
mother and son were whirled up to the constellations as mom bear and
baby bear. They are now happy, and playing together, but who knows.
Maybe they're frozen in combat, still unclear as to who they are to each
other.

BOY
You see, over there, that's the mom's head, that's baby's foot.

JESSIEE
I'm pretty sure the mom bear was running to hug her child,
not to trash him.

BOY
How would you know?

JESSIEE
I know, I'm a girl, I have maternal instincts.
Now it's time to go to my mom's bedroom and have sex.

BOY
Is that a maternal instinct too?

JESSIEE
Maybe. Come on, Benji, my mom will be back in like an hour.

BOY
We should have our own star story. What would it be?

JESSIEE
Come on, Benji. Benji.
Hoi Ben. Benjamin. Benjamino.
Boink.

BOY
Boink back.

JESSIEE
Double boink.

BOY
Jessie stop it I'm trying to concentrate.

JESSIEE
Benji... [let's go to my parents' bedroom and have sex.]

BOY
Again? It's like all you ever want to do now.
Jessie I love you but sometimes I'm sorry we discovered sex.

KAHEKILI
Cold? You got like chicken skin. We go fo' swim in da watah, neh, in da watah, warm da bodies stay.

JESSIEE
I don't usually swim.

KAHEKILI
I t'ink today da day fo' doing t'ings you not usually do.

[Handwritten marginalia:] HAHAHA / Boink back?! Where did that come from? / Is it a game / I used to play FIVE? / when I love plays / Babysitting / TJ a very / Interesting / Entertaining / Humiliating / Interesting / activity / Revisiting

                    JESSIEE
No.

                    KAHEKILI
You good? You lookin' da kine.

                    JESSIEE
Da what?

                    KAHEKILI
Like you look at me but you not see me.

                    JESSIEE
Yeh, Sorry, I just, no I'm fine.
I don't like large masses of water, it,
freaks me out. How it, um,
how it keeps moving all the time,
oh my god all this sand, I am covered in sand.

                    KAHEKILI
Da beach, lotta sand, y'know, how it is.

                    JESSIEE
I'm, sand. Too much sand.
Drink. I think a drink!
Is it too early or too late?
It's Maui, I'm sure something will be open.

                    KAHEKILI
Nah. I neva drink.

                    JESSIEE
Eh? I don't swim, you don't drink, clearly we're not
meant to be together. Come on, it's a special night.
Where's the night scene happenin' in this town -

                    KAHEKILI
Haw, slow slow, Miss Nicole. Da sun be up soon, no bar
open anywhere on dis island.
An' even if deh be, I couldn't get in.

                    JESSIEE
You blacklisted or something?

                    KAHEKILI
What, no! Under-aged.

[Handwritten annotations in margin: "Sex on the beach = Sand in everywhere. Sand in your hair, eyes, ears, belly button - Expect to find sand in your ass crack DAYS after event." "have decided to not worth it."]

JESSIEE
Huh.

KAHEKILI
What.

JESSIEE
How under-aged.

KAHEKILI
Fifteen.

JESSIEE
Huh.

KAHEKILI
What?

JESSIEE
Of course.

KAHEKILI
Nicole. What, li'dat, haw wait Nicole.

JESSIEE
Don't wait Nicole me, you're fifteen.
I've just committed a crime. I mean,
unless Maui years are like dog years to Ohio years.

KAHEKILI
Wha? Nicole, wait, for real, you go you go? Nicole!

JESSIEE
My name is not Nicole! Also, stop talking to me!

KAHEKILI
For real?

JESSIEE
For real what.

KAHEKILI
For real stop? Dass it?
One number change everyt'ing you see?

JESSIEE
You are fifteen. That is a big number for me, okay?

KAHEKILI
Her problem my age, y'know?
Dass like, I can't jus' tek back, say,
actually no, I'm sixteen,
or some odda number dat mek you feel better.
So I jus' say,
Kay den. What is your name, Nicole. Real name.

JESSIEE
Jessiee. With two ees.

KAHEKILI
You have good time in Maui, kay, Jessiee with two ees?
Aloha.
I'm t'inking, no need, y'know?
I'm a man a da watah,
no need fo' no woman li'dat, yah?

JESSIEE
And he just stands up, dusts off his butt and starts to leave.

KAHEKILI
I come fo' ride da breaks,
no need some crazy *haole* lady who look for "happiness."

JESSIEE
I'm sitting there like what just happened,
but also don't go don't go,
don't go pretty man with pretty hands
after all what is a number it's just a number,
no the number is fifteen you do not get to perv out on fifteen –

KAHEKILI
But befo' I know what when how,

JESSIEE
Suddenly he turns, walks back to me,

KAHEKILI
My mout' opens and say,
I dive fo' Black Rock ritual tonight.
Come. Tek pictures.
An' den buy me my drink, neh?

KAHEKILI (cont)
An' I'm like,
Haw. Not bad brah.
An' befo' she say no or yes,
I turn around and shoot straight da odda way.

JESSIEE
I watch his silhouette shrink into a dot
His unbelievably hot, stop it, fifteen-year-old dot.
I put my shirt back on, switch the crazy off and decide, sleep.

GUIDEBOOK
Be sure to secure accommodations before you arrive! For the full treatment, Maui resorts can't be beat when visiting Hawaii. Living in ultimate island luxury may keep you from ever leaving the property, until the bill comes.

(As hotel front desk.)
I'm sorry ma'am. The only vacancy at this time is our deluxe Oceanfront suite available to you at the Endless Escape Rate of $519 a night. How long are you planning to stay with us?

Jessiee gives him a credit card.

JESSIEE
I still feel this boy all over.
I still feel his hands all over.
Tanned, rough on the outside soft on the inside,
And I'm like, stop it Jessiee, stop re-feeling the teenager's hands, his slowly pulsing, grating but not too much, rough-ish smooth-ish,

GUIDEBOOK *(As hotel front desk)*
I am very sorry ma'am but it seems your card is not going through?

Jessiee gives him another credit card.

JESSIEE
Fingers! His hands had fingers. Boys back home, no fingers, it's like grope grope, smoosh and squish, but oh fingers. Touching, lingering, not just passing through to get to home base, fingers...

GUIDEBOOK *(As hotel front desk.)*
I apologize ma'am but,

Jessiee gives him another credit card.

JESSIEE
I have an obsession with hands. Like, obsession.
If I could I would build a shrine of hands.

GUIDEBOOK
(As hotel front desk.) Excellent. Your bill will be available upon checkout.
Complimentary breakfast is served in our open air Black Rock Terrace at
seven a.m., elevators to your left. Have a wonderful stay.

JESSIEE
Just, tells you so much about a person.
Is this a hand that's known more dishwater or office paper.
Have these fingers spent more time curled into fists
or sifting through someone's hair.
Is this a grip that will clutch at your heart or at your throat.
Or both.
Or neither.
Just by touch you know.
You know?

Jessiee looks at the Boy, who has maybe laid his head on her lap.

BOY
I think it's a little pervie.
I mean yeh hands are great and they let you do stuff, but you?
You get all focused and intense when you talk about hands,
and I'm telling you it gets a little pervie sometimes. It's like
sometimes I think, is Jessiee gonna creep up on me one night
chop off my hands and run away with them,
coz actually that's all she wants from me?

JESSIEE
His hands were a little different, though.
A tender pair of hands,
a pair that hadn't gone through enough of its life
to have worn much of its owner's stories.
I can't imagine what those hands might look like today,
how they might casually rest on the driver's steering wheel,
finger a cigarette or two, sooth their master's chin with a cool aftershave.

BOY
My hands are real big for a ninth grader.
I should take up something, guitar or basketball,
something where big hands are appreciated.

JESSIEE
I appreciate them.

BOY
Just when they do stuff for you.

KAHEKILI
Haw, bruh, I get home t'row my board up against da wall
an' tek some ice for dis my *ule*.
Li'dat my little man, I wen rub him up against some serious grains a sand
nuh, buggah be purple! UGH!
Shoots, bruh, da ocean,
she always ready wid some new kine da painful stuff.
But I love dis. My purple penis, neh?
Da hurt mek you into somet'ing else nah?
Y'scrap some, y'bleed some,
an' da blood from da scrap, get you goin', get you harder, get you stronger,
till you know you strong enough fo' tek off da shirt
an' scrap wid da big bruddas out deh.
NAH? NAH? Ha.
Yeh, deh I stay wid dis pack a frozen broccoli rollin' over my *ule*, my fadda
come home wid a new pile a scrap wood and da stink a death on his face.
We don't even talk now, not even.
Li'dat, he see his dinner on his boy's balls
an' he just pass on by, li'dat.
Jus' li'dat. Pass on by.
Shoots brah, like I wanna talk with him, neh?
Nah. Forget about it.

JESSIEE
What happened to the science project?

BOY
Which one?

JESSIEE
You were building a sky with milk cartons and a toothpick,
with those fighting bears –

BOY
Oh yeh, switched up for lemon lamplight.
Don't you remember, I smelled like lemons for two weeks.
Why?

JESSIEE

Just wondering.

BOY

Makes me nervous when you start wondering things, Jessie. You never just wonder things.

JESSIEE

I don't?

BOY

Nope. What's up.

JESSIEE

No. Nothing. Forget about it.

KAHEKILI

Jus' li'dat. Pass on by.
But y'know, what would I say, if he ass about my *ule*.
Fadda man, I wen stick dis little man in one *haole* lady at da beach, Jessiee, wid two ees,
wid her boring bag an' her biode-chamacallit blood sponge t'ing,
an' your boy don't know how fo' stop t'inking about dis lady,
an' I don't know maybe she be my wife she be my family.
What you t'ink about dat, eh?
Yeh Fadda man anodda t'ing I got that you don't got. Li'dat, Fadda you make me sick how not'ing you are, like I wanna say dat?
I'd chop off all ten a my toes to get myself anodda fadda who taller den me, like I wanna say dat?
Shoots brah, like I wanna say dat?
He not hard enough to hear dat.

JESSIEE

It's not fair.

BOY

What now?

JESSIEE

It wasn't their fault, either of them.

BOY

Whose fault? What?

JESSIEE

The bears.

BOY

Bears.

JESSIEE

It wasn't their fault, they didn't know enough,
they had the right to try and protect themselves, you know?
People have the right to draw an arrow
on a bear running towards them
or to whup the shit out of a hunter trying to kill them,
people have a right to protect themselves from harm.
It's not okay that we're all glad that this big cosmic dick came and intervened, whipped them up into balls of gas in the sky not even as people, but as bears, and that's the good part, it's just not fair.

BOY

Jessie. Tell me what's wrong.

JESSIEE

Everything.

BOY

Just pick one and tell me.

JESSIEE

I'm pregnant.
But, no more sad things.
Maui! Beach Sex! Clean bed!
I check in, close the blinds, take a pill and check the fuck out!

GUIDEBOOK

The Legend of Lele Kawa on Black Rock Cliff. Legend tells us the last chief of Maui, Kahekili proved his spiritual strength by leaping from sacred Pu'u Keka'a to the Pacific.

Boom. Drum.

KAHEKILI & JESSIEE

I wake with a start,

JESSIEE

Where the hell am I?

                KAHEKILI
                                              I musta wen tek one nap,

                JESSIEE
Can't tell if it's day or night,

                KAHEKILI
                Don't know if dat sun be coming or going?

                GUIDEBOOK
As the sun begins his slow dive into the ocean, torch lighting signals the start of a nightly ritual of Lele Kawa on Black Rock Cliff.

                JESSIEE
I've slept through the day,

                KAHEKILI
                                              I am late,

                JESSIEE
Am I late? Did I miss him?

                GUIDEBOOK *(as ritual Emcee)*
With sunset painting the sky, a young cliff diver honors his heritage by re-tracing footsteps in the sand on Ka'anapali Beach.

                JESSIEE
                Sorry, hi, where's the diving thing happening?

                GUIDEBOOK *(as ritual Emcee)*
A chant of old Hawai'i begins the progression of our warrior;

                JESSIEE
                Hello, excuse me, I'm looking for Black Rock?
                Some kind of diving?

                GUIDEBOOK *(as ritual Emcee)*
The echo of the conch shell announces his arrival.

    Conch shell blows.

                JESSIEE
There he was.

GUIDEBOOK *(as ritual Emcee)*
He leaves a trail of glowing torches surrounding the lagoon as he makes his way to Black Rock.

JESSIEE
Tiny man atop the cliff,
like the tiny frog on my index finger,

GUIDEBOOK *(as ritual Emcee)*
Upon reaching the summit, he offers his flaming torch to the ocean below,

JESSIEE
There he was.

GUIDEBOOK
Casts his flower *lei* into the sea;

JESSIEE
At the edge of the cliff.

GUIDEBOOK
And finally takes the breathtaking dive,

JESSIEE
Staring out into the –

GUIDEBOOK
From Black Rock into the rolling surf below

The diver leaps off the

JESSIEE
No!

Drum. Boom.

BOY
We should name him Benjamin after me.

JESSIEE
We could also name him Jessie after me.

BOY
Jessie is a girl name.

JESSIEE
It can be a boy name.
Also we don't know Jessie is a boy. Could be a girl.

BOY
Oh, if he's a girl then we should name her Jasmin.
Half of your name, half of mine.

JESSIEE
Jasmin's a Disney princess.

BOY
Okay, then Bessie, half of my name, half of –

JESSIEE
Bessie's a cow.

BOY
Hey. Why you so cranky?

JESSIEE
I'm not. I just, can't believe we're gonna do this. It's crazy.

BOY
No it's not. People had babies in their teens all the time.

JESSIEE
Those people didn't have to take SATs.

BOY
You still wanna do that, huh?

JESSIEE
Maybe.

BOY
We'll figure it out. My mom will help,
we could get a tutor or something, you could live with us,

JESSIEE
You told her?!

BOY
'Course not. Not yet. We're gonna have to, at some point.

JESSIEE
She's gonna make us get rid of it. I know my mom will.

BOY
We could run away? We could run away some place far, like Robinson Crusoe, to an island,

JESSIEE
Robinson Crusoe was shipwrecked, Benji.

BOY
Then – I mean, whatever, we can still go to an island. We could go to Hawaii. I could catch things in the sea, teach Jasmin how to hula,

JESSIEE
You know how to hula?

BOY
I could learn while she is growing up.

JESSIEE
Girl hula and boy hula is different.

BOY
I'll learn how to girl hula. For Jasmin.
And also boy hula, if it's a Benjamin.

JESSIEE
All of this is a really horrible plan.

BOY
You have no romantic notions.

JESSIEE
I have a thing growing in me yes I have no romantic notions.
I have a thing growing in me. It's been growing. Benjamin.
It's gonna keep growing.

BOY
I know.

JESSIEE
It's been over two months, I don't think they can even –

                              BOY
Well we're not doing that.

                             JESSIEE
Well we're not going to Hawaii.

                              BOY
You're so serious. It's like I don't even know you any more.
Jess I love you but sometimes I'm sorry we discovered sex.

                             JESSIEE
Ben I love you but sometimes I wish you'd fucking grow up.

A loud splash, a body thrown into a mass of water.

                           GUIDEBOOK
Be sure to enjoy this nightly tradition at the poolside Cliff Dive Bar at
Sheraton Maui.

Jessiee waits.

                             JESSIEE
He does this for a living, there's no way anything would happen,
even if it did what do I care, I just met him,
barely met him barely a one night stand, illegal one night stand,
I shouldn't even be here,
but I sit here, I keep scanning the horizon,
squinting, searching for a head bobbing up and down.
Still no head.

Do you do that?
That thing where you have images of,
blades slashing your hands when you blend a smoothie,
buses smashing into your ribs when you step off the sidewalk,
volcanic rocks splitting into your head when you jump off a cliff.

Still no head.

I'm thinking nothing's wrong, calm the fuck down.
But you know, it's like reflex a self-defense thing,
where when something bad might happen, even if that "might" is a
miniscule little fraction of a possibility, your mind jumps to that
image, savors that image, lets that image *be*, in your head, so when you
find out that your mom's legs will be chopped off you could be like oh
phew, I thought she was gonna die a slow and smelly death while she
bankrupts the entire world, wheelchair? Sure I can deal with that.

JESSIEE (cont)
I can deal with a lot of things, just gotta make it seem not as bad as the really bad thing. But if the thought of the really bad thing – even when it's not real, not real at all, still makes you feel icky and vomitty and just green in the face almost as bad as if it were real, then what's the point, is there a point, still no head!
Where's the head?
Did he float up a corpse and nobody can see coz it's so dark? How'd it get so dark, so soon, the sun Just set!
I should call the police, maybe I'm the only one who was really watching,
maybe he's a gun for hire, light the torch, jump the cliff, job well done and nobody cares, maybe I'm his only hope for a decent burial before he's ripped up into shark / food –

KAHEKILI
Hi.

JESSIEE
Aaaaaaaaaaaaaaaaaaaaaaaaaaaaaaaaaaaarrrrrrrgh!

KAHEKILI
...

JESSIEE
How did you get here.

KAHEKILI
I – You okay?

JESSIEE
There was no head.

KAHEKILI
There was no head...?

JESSIEE
I was watching this whole time. For your head.
You never came up. How'd you, I didn't even see,
My God don't you ever do that again.

KAHEKILI
I swim around da rock fo' get back.
Ritual, ceremony, everyt'ing very beautiful, y'know,
nobody gon' wanna see da help. Kill da magic.
I am sorry fo' mek you worry.
–

KAHEKILI (cont)
It is nice, t'ough. Dat I mek someone worry.

A moment.
Phone rings.

GUIDEBOOK *(As hotel bellboy)*
Sorry to interrupt, ma'am, but you have a call waiting at the front desk.

No.

JESSIEE
And then a week went by. Learnt things about Maui.
Things people generally learn about new places in a week,

GUIDEBOOK
Drive along the road to sanctuary
Watch the waters fall in harmony
Nature's Kahuna: The Road to Hana

KAHEKILI
Chiiiiiiiiiiiiiiiiiiii-ho!

JESSIEE
Chiiiiiiiiiiiiiiiiiiii-ho! Faster! Faster! Faster!

KAHEKILI
Dis plenny fast, Jessiee.

JESSIEE
Aw is baby scared? Does baby want me to drive?

KAHEKILI
It's li'dat, huh? Kay den Jessiee wid two ees,
you about to t'row up all kine stuff –
Ae Ae Ae / Chiiiiiiiiiiiiiiiiiiii-ho!

JESSIEE
Chiiiiiiiiiiiiiiiiiiii-ho!

GUIDEBOOK
Gotta take your tine with turns and trials
With 54 bridges and 600 curves in 50 miles
Oh you don't wanna speed down to Hana

Jessiee throws up.

KAHEKILI
Shoots, you good? Jessiee.

JESSIEE
No worries I'm totally – [fine.]

Jessiee tries to not throw up.

KAHEKILI
Here, tek some coconut watah, yah? Mek you feel –

Jessiee throws up on him.

GUIDEBOOK
Find a spot to read while getting tanned
Find the shore of softest whitest sand
Come to Napili: Finest in Maui

KAHEKILI
You come beach, you go watah.
I don't understand dis come beach fo' read book, Jessiee.

JESSIEE
It's what grown-ups like to do.
You'll understand when you are older.

Kahekili takes book, reads.

KAHEKILI.
"...He sucks each of my nipples hard, then follows the line of ice cream down my –" Ice cream?

JESSIEE
For some people.

Awkward.

JESSIEE (cont)
Oh my god, what the hell is that.
Is that a sea lion, I think it's a sea lion!

GUIDEBOOK
A monk seal might find his way to short
Soaking in the adoration for
(Monk seal singing sounds "Arp arp arp.")
Wildlife of Maui

[handwritten margin note: have to thank Tim Hassler for this brilliant monk seal arping idea]

JESSIEE
Oooh helllooo purty purty.

KAHEKILI
No, no touch!

JESSIEE
Why? Does it bite?

KAHEKILI
It is illegal.

JESSIEE
You're illegal.
Come on, can I at least take a picture with him?

KAHEKILI
Haw, tourists.

JESSIEE
Don't be such a local. Embrace the touristy!
The world is so beautiful!

GUIDEBOOK
Volcanic mountains rise up to the skies
Frozen Lava hums the lullabies
Don't miss the sunrise at Hale'akala

JESSIEE
It's five fucking a.m.

KAHEKILI
You tole me you want fo' see da sunrise.

JESSIEE
Out my hotel window, in bed sipping coffee.

KAHEKILI
You stay such da tourist, you must embrace da local.

GUIDEBOOK
Weather can be unpredictable
Ten thousand feet above sea level ...

                        JESSIEE
I can't feel my face I can't feel my face.

                        KAHEKILI
            Say cheese,

                        JESSIEE
You say cheese I can't fucking feel my fucking face.

                        KAHEKILI
Hele mai. Come fo' me.

Hugs her into his windbreaker.
She burrows her face into his chest.
Jessiee inaudibly rants displeasure and general
early morning crankiness from his chest.

                        KAHEKILI
            Eh, look.

Jessiee peaks out from his jacket.
The sun is rising over the clouds.

                        JESSIEE
            Oh – Wow.

They take it in.

                        KAHEKILI
Hale'akala, House of da Sun.

They look on for a good while.
They really want to kiss.

A phone rings.

            GUIDEBOOK *(As hotel bellboy)*
Sorry to interrupt but there's a call awaiting you at the front desk, ma'am.

    No.

                        JESSIEE
There was a lot of no sex happening.
My little travel package was like, "Oh come ooooooooon, seriously?
We're in Maui it is Mutual the age of consent in Maui is Sixteen
(fifteen if you count the year in the womb)..."

JESSIEE (cont)
But. Yeh. No. We did touristy things, and extreme sports things, and other grown-up things, like,
>Drink! Drink! Drink! Drink! Drink!

KAHEKILI
>Da drink be pink! I do not drink any kine pinky drinkie.

JESSIEE
>It's just champagne, God, you're so fifteen.

KAHEKILI.
>It's li'dat? Kay den.
(Drinks.)
>Haw. Dis nasty. Taste like rotten soda, but jus' pink.

JESSIEE
Few sips later –

KAHEKILI
>Da waterman, y'know?
>Da waterman, da waterman,
>Duke Kahanamoku, Tom Blake, Roger Erikson!
>My bruddas! Faddas! Idols.
>Jessiee dey be da Gods a da ocean!
>Jessiee, watch, neh,
>soon I be da God a da, somet'ing.
>Or everyt'ing.

GUIDEBOOK
Boasting total mastery of all oceanic endeavors, the revered waterman can fish, dive, surf, windsurf, kayak, bodysurf, interpret complex weather data, and save the odd drowning man, every now and then. If need be, he can survive entirely on self- harvested ocean bounty, spearing his food from the nearby reefs.

KAHEKILI
>I am mini waterman, I know da ocean, she know me,
>but we da kine y'know, not yet really know, neh?
>Haw my fadda, he know da ocean, he da kine da any kine
>bout da ocean, but li'dat he go he go he go, like,
>neva he know da ocean, like neva he care.
>He sit deh, wid da small block a wood he mek into
>smaller block a dis turtle, neh,
>he know and I know he da smallest buggah on dis island.

KAHEKILI (cont)
I wen outgrow my fadda long time ago.
Me, I gon' stay one a da Gods.

GUIDEBOOK
Generally built like a tank and typically soft- spoken (choosing to let his actions do the talking), he's a bit of a loner.

KAHEKILI
An' den da *haole* piece of shit ass leave
one dollar fifty-two cent for tip, an' I am fuck you!
Sometimes, da kine, suck, y'know?
I like da watah. I jus' wanna go watah.
I hate people.
People suck.
You I like.
I like you.
Don't go.

GUIDEBOOK
Watermen fear neither tempest nor shark and rarely head for higher ground. It's really not for any and every little Hawaiian boy.

KAHEKILI
Marry me.

GUIDEBOOK
[Ukulele strum] !!

JESSIEE
Not yet.

KAHEKILI
Marry me.

GUIDEBOOK
[Ukulele strum] !!

JESSIEE
We're not there yet.

KAHEKILI
Marry me! Jessiee with two ees. Marry me.

GUIDEBOOK
[Ukulele strum] !!
[Ukulele strum] !!

KAHEKILI
I ask her, marry me.
Marry me, Jessiee with two ees, marry me. And she say,
And she say,
She say,

JESSIEE
Sure Why not.

KAHEKILI
Yes?!

JESSIEE
No! Yes! I don't know!

KAHEKILI
Why?

JESSIEE
Because you're – and I'm –
Because it's crazy and impossible and
are you even allowed to get married?

KAHEKILI
How dat matter? I love you.

JESSIEE
It's a lot more complicated than that.

KAHEKILI
Because why? Jus', I must live wid you fo'eva.
Jus' I love you.

JESSIEE
It's not that simple. You're young.
You don't understand what it means to –

KAHEKILI
I don't like dis. We tek it back, neh?

[handwritten annotations:]
I am such a sucker for alternate narratives!
I know it's annoying plot device for some people
But I say give me annoying alternatives
over No alternatives!
Any day! I like having options.

GUIDEBOOK
Watermen fear neither tempest nor shark and rarely head for higher ground. It's really not for any and every little Hawaiian boy.

> KAHEKILI
> One week wen go by. Learnt t'ings about Jessiee.
> T'ings people generally learn about new people in
>
> one week, maybe little more than dat.

GUIDEBOOK
Jessiee on women's rights:

> JESSIEE
> Look. If you need to chop off your boobs because it's gonna kill you, it's up to the owner of boob to chop or not chop. But when it comes to the thing in your womb, all of a sudden it's up to the – what?

> KAHEKILI
> Did you chop off your, [boobs]?

> JESSIEE
> Ha, why, did they feel fake to you?

Boobs.

Awkward.

> KAHEKILI
> Look, brah, I was just t'inking,
> I hope you neva chop off anyt'ing.
> Life so different after you do that, eh,
> go chop somet'ing off,
> ocean smell different,
> rain fall different,
> food taste different.

> JESSIEE
> What did you chop off to know so much?

> KAHEKILI
> My boobs.

GUIDEBOOK
Jessiee on names:

JESSIEE
– And after the petition is filed, you get a hearing
at the civil court, and if it's granted, you get a new
social security card, which you need to take to the DMV
to get your license changed, also passport, voter regis–

KAHEKILI
All a dat for jus' one more "e"? Dass crazy.

JESSIEE
She thought I needed to feel I don't know special.

KAHEKILI
I t'ink I gon' change my name too. Hello, I am Kahekili
with fifty-two "i"s. I am special. I am fifty-two "i"s more
special den you. Jessiee's modda say so.

JESSIEE
Jessiee's modda say a lot of things.
Jessiee's modda gonna say a whole lot of really
pissed off things when Jessiee gets back on the grid.

KAHEKILI
Yah? When Jessiee doin' dat?

JESSIEE
When she sells all her dope.

GUIDEBOOK
Jessiee on family relationships:

JESSIEE
I mean, I love her, she's my best friend, but sometimes,
my mom she's such a fucking loser,
you know what I mean?
Hello, you have cancer, you have no insurance,
maybe call your only child about it so we can do
something before they take your legs away?
Cut to: four surgeries later, she's lame, I'm bankrupt,
both survived to tell the tale of how you wish you hadn't.

KAHEKILI
Where's your fadda?

JESSIEE
Who knows. Who cares. Where's your mom?

He shrugs.

KAHEKILI
I t'ink one modda is bettah den one fadda.
I wish I had one, even if she one loser.
I would trade my loser fadda for a loser modda anyday.

JESSIEE
I could be your loser mom.

KAHEKILI
I t'ink you too old to be my modda.

JESSIEE
Ha, them fightin' words, brah?

KAHEKILI
You know, if you my modda,
I mus' go wid when you leave.

JESSIEE
To Akron?

KAHEKILI
To anywheh.
In Hawaii, the son mus' protect his family.
Wheh you go, I come wid.

JESSIEE
Maybe. That would be nice.
Although, you wouldn't last very long.
Akron is landlocked.

KAHEKILI.
What's dat?

JESSIEE
No water. Just land.

A phone rings.

GUIDEBOOK *(As hotel bellboy)*
Excuse me ma'am you have a call awaiting you at the front desk.

No.

JESSIEE
What next? What next? Mountain!
Can we go up the mountain?
Can we bike up the mountain?
Laugh my ass off I would die of asphyxiation within
the first mile. AHHHHH who the fuck cares.
I love this fucking place.

KAHEKILI
I like her talk, her excited talk, eh.

A phone rings.

GUIDEBOOK *(As hotel bellboy)*
For you, ma'am. The gentleman says it is urgent?

No.

JESSIEE
Read me something?
I don't know, anything, like read the menu.
I just fucking love your accent. Li'dat, bruh!

KAHEKILI
Me an' her talk so different
but li'dat, like pingpong game, neh,
she go I go she go I go, li'dat, like bam bam bam bam,
so easy so quick so fun
I neva know talk so much joy.
I talk wid her and I say t'ings I would neva say.
I do t'ings I neva do neva done.

A phone rings.

GUIDEBOOK *(As hotel bellboy)*
Family emergency, ma'am. Are you sure you would like to decline?

KAHEKILI
I do da t'ings an' I t'ink
dis da most stupid t'ing I eva done,
tekin' pictures readin' books,
drinkin' some stupid drinks like I my fadda or what, driving up da
mountain fo' see da fuckin' sunrise I know I can see bigger an' warmer
riding da breaks on my own.
Ho, dis boy not see his board fo' like da whole week. Da whole week, my

KAHEKILI (cont)
board dryin' up against da wall, an' I don't even miss it.
Not even.

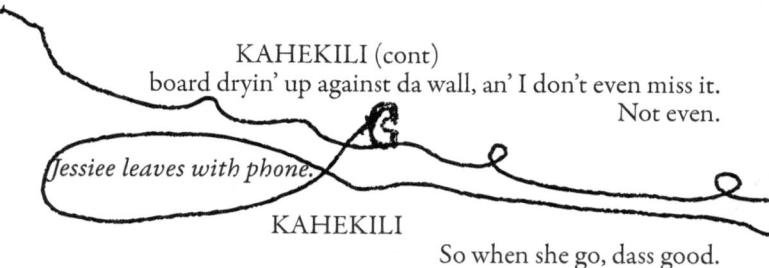

Jessiee leaves with phone.

KAHEKILI
So when she go, dass good.
Yah?
She go back fo' her grid, I go back fo' my board,
dis pingpong all dis shit, jus' some fun dass it. Dass all.
No way I leave da ocean, da breaks, da dream of waterman, fo' dis
pingpong talk dat mek me not me? No way I leave my board my Maui,
fo' go live wid Jessiee on her grid wheh deh stay no ocean?
Fo' go live wid dis dream lady who hate da watah love da mountains.
Even if she ask,
Even if she like wanna be my wife my family,
Dass jus' *lolo*,
Right?

JESSIEE
Hi, hey. Sorry about that.

KAHEKILI
Everyt'ing good?

JESSIEE
Sure, yeh. Just um, something back home,

KAHEKILI
Home?

JESSIEE
Not, I'm, home. Stuff. Things.
I think I have to leave this –

KAHEKILI
Na nah na nah na nah na nah, da international police,
find you out, neh? Haw, I tole you Jessiee wid two ees,
you / gonna get buss up,

JESSIEE
What? No it's not – it's not / funny, stop it Kahekili,
I'm not kidding.

KAHEKILI
Tole you about dose credit card trails, neh?

JESSIEE
What the hell are you – will you please –

KAHEKILI
Now dey come at you, we gotta swim now,
we gotta swim away, yeh? I'll / save you,
I'll save you, Jessiee wid two –

JESSIEE
Are you drunk I said shut the fuck up!
Sorry.
Just, something just fucking –
No more [sad things].
Hey, let's do something different.

KAHEKILI
Kay.

JESSIEE
Let's go somewhere crazy. Like way way way.
Let's go up the cliff.
Black Rock!

KAHEKILI
I climb up Black Rock every odda day,
dass not da somewhere crazy.
But if you want, we go climb up first t'ing tomorrow.

JESSIEE
No right now. Like, now, this moment.

KAHEKILI
Jessiee it's midnight.

JESSIEE
Yeh I know. Like I said, crazy!
I wanna make love to you in the dark
on the jagged rocks of the blackest cliff –

BOY
It's like all you ever wanna do now.
Sometimes I'm sorry we discovered sex.

KAHEKILI
You can not go up deh in dis dark, Jessiee.
It is illegal. It uh da kine too dangerous, neh?

JESSIEE
Stop being such a fifteen-year-old.

BOY
We could run away?

KAHEKILI
I don't know Jessiee,

BOY
We could run away some place far,
like Robinson Crusoe, to an island,

KAHEKILI
I t'ink maybe da better t'ing, go tomorrow morning.
Come now.

JESSIEE
No, I really need to,

BOY
Jessie!

KAHEKILI
Jessiee, da whole week, you neva even dip one
toe in da watah, now you go up da cliff
surrounded all by da sea?
Try t'ink t'rough what you gon' do befo'
we pull ourselves in fo' sumt'ing *lolo*, yah?

JESSIEE
Okay fine, you puss out, I'll climb up by myself.

KAHEKILI
Kay den, you go you go, kay, shoots, go yourself, fine,
you t'ink I care? You go you go, go knock your head open
some place stupid in da dark by yourself. Jessiee.

She's gone.

                          BOY
        Jessie!

                        KAHEKILI
            Jessiee?

                          BOY
        Jessie! Jessie!

                         JESSIEE
I'm climbing this cliff right now.
Needs a lot of concentration, lot, of, pep, good things good though!

                          BOY
        Jessie!

                         JESSIEE
I am in Maui, all the way in Maui, I am happy, no
more sad things. No more sad things!

                          BOY
        Jessie!

                         JESSIEE
Happy happy happy.

                          BOY
        Jessie!

                         JESSIEE
Eye of the beholder.

                          BOY
        Jessie!

                         JESSIEE
Oh my god what!

                          BOY
        How?

                         JESSIEE
What you mean how, I don't know how,
I was knocked out for the whole process.

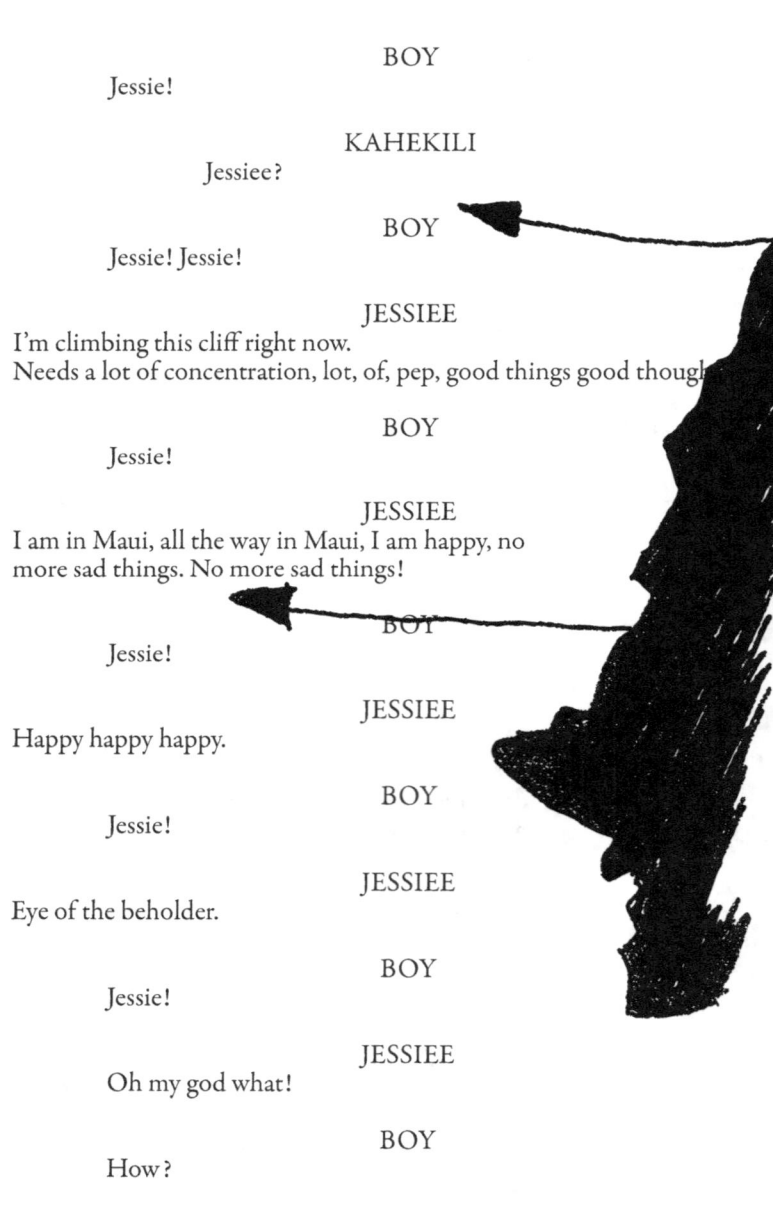

BOY

Jessie.

JESSIEE

Mom.

BOY

You told her?!

JESSIEE

She found the sonogram. She booked the, thing.

BOY

When?

JESSIEE

Yesterday.

BOY

Is it gone, the whole thing?

JESSIEE

No just the odd leg and arm of course the whole thing!

BOY

Why did you do it.

JESSIEE

Benji, come on now we weren't gonna –

BOY

No, you weren't gonna. I had a say, I had a right, I had –
I was gonna learn girl hula, You can't kill someone and be –

JESSIEE

I didn't kill anyone! It was gonna kill me!

BOY

You can't kill someone and be done with it.
They become something else, they become stars, air bubbles,

JESSIEE

Those are stories, Benjamin, Oh my god,

BOY

They become something else and we won't know him he won't

BOY (cont)
know us, like Arcas never knew Callisto, and we'll meet one day,
and he's gonna shoot us without ever knowing,

JESSIEE
It's just a myth Benji.
You can't expect me to give up my life for a myth.

BOY
You gave up my child for SATs.

JESSIEE
That's not fair. It's not that simple.
You're young. You don't understand what it means to have a life.

BOY
Do you? Goodbye, Jessie.

Boy leaves.

JESSIEE
The things you lose sometimes stay.
The scar, the stump, the phantom limb,
the the the not-there-anymore-ness of it becomes a hole and it stays,
– time! They say time helps but actually you know what, it doesn't this is what time does,
time
creates other crap other stumps scars,
piles new sad on to old sad,
you fake forget about the old sad – like pain distraction, slapping your face makes you forget about the tummy ache for a bit kind of thing?

KAHEKILI
Jessiee!

JESSIEE
But all of the things, all of the sad things,

KAHEKILI
Jessiee!

JESSIEE
They stay.

JESSIEE (cont)
Pool,
flood over,
into some terrifying ocean of lost things.

GUIDEBOOK
Ka'anapali

KAHEKILI
                                        There she was.

JESSIEE
But we ignore this ocean.

GUIDEBOOK
Ka'anapali

KAHEKILI
                                Tiny girl at tip a da cliff,

JESSIEE
Look away and hope.

GUIDEBOOK
Where the waves are young and free

KAHEKILI
    Jessiee!

JESSIEE
Hope, maybe the sad thing will drown and die in your ocean.

KAHEKILI
Jessiee, come down fo' me, neh?

JESSIEE
But it doesn't.

GUIDEBOOK
Ka'anapali

JESSIEE
(To Guidebook) Stop.

Guidebook stops singing.

                    KAHEKILI
              Okay, I'm coming deh.

                    JESSIEE
It grows, waiting.

                    KAHEKILI
              Wait, okay? I'm coming deh.

                    JESSIEE
Waiting 'til you're on a cliff surrounded by the sea.

                    KAHEKILI
              Full moon tonight, you not gon' win da breaks, Jessiee,

                    JESSIEE
Leaving your sick mom coz you're mad at her,

                    KAHEKILI
              It gon' for sure break you.

                    JESSIEE
Mad at her for making you do things you weren't sure you wanted to do,
for getting sick for leaving,

                    KAHEKILI
        Jessiee!

                    JESSIEE
Mad coz they say it's better to be mad,
coz a new sad will make all the old sad feel new all over again.

                    KAHEKILI
                    She turn her face fo' da watah an',

                    JESSIEE
All this water, I smell all this ocean,

                    KAHEKILI
                    I know what come next, I know,

                    JESSIEE
And I see this boy calling, climbing,

KAHEKILI
I climb da rocks, I climb dees rocks I climb
fucking every odda day,
but da breaks, been over da rocks, mek dem slippery,

JESSIEE
But all I could think,

KAHEKILI
I gon' lose her,

JESSIEE
The only thought I can think is,

KAHEKILI
Don't lose her, don't lose her Kahekili,
Jessiee!

JESSIEE
No More.

KAHEKILI
I'm here, Jessiee.

JESSIEE
Just, no more.

KAHEKILI
I came fo' you, right?

JESSIEE
You do not get to run away from this any more.

KAHEKILI
No!

A leap.

Part of your Body

Girl met a boy / showed him the world / offered her hands to hold / In the swirl / He messed up her bed / Eager he said / softly / "All of my universe is here in your face / let me know your eyes / warm as the sun / mold your secrets / deep as your heart / Trace your lips / till night turns to morning / don't need a lot / let me be part of your body (splash)

Boy met a girl / Gave her the stars / offered the moon / venus and mars / she messed up his bed / she said softly / palms let me know your fingers / soft as the sun / hold your flaws / big as your heart / Trace your arms / till night turns to morning / don't need the stars

A loud splash, a body thrown into a mass of water.

KAHEKILI

> Dis dream, dis lady,
> da waves da breaks dey eat up dis lady.
> But dis time I fly after her, I can ass da ocean fo' give lady back,
> dis time not dream,
> dis da real t'ing,

JESSIEE

Frogs, thousands of them,
but they were dead, taken care of,
and there's this one little frog, cute even, singing to me, lulling me to
Maui, it was a good feeling. It was a good dream.
When the nurse woke me up, he was like, I'm sorry but you can't sleep
on the cafeteria floor,
while eyeballing this guidebook that had been serving as a headrest.
I'm like, dude, my mom's on her fourth surgery, our entire life savings
belong to you now,
I'm allowed to borrow a past-season guidebook to lean on while I
fucking nap on whichever fucking surface I fucking choose to nap on,
no?
I didn't say that.
I wiped my drool, mumbled something about
I'm sorry I'm tired and went back to Mom.
Back to Mom. Just Mom and me.

KAHEKILI

> Jus' me and da ocean.
> I swim I swim I swim,
> I stroke and stroke and stroke.
> It's like da ocean, she jealous of my pingpong talk an' decide,
> out odda fucking blue she gon' tek her again.
> I look I look I look fo' da head, I know dis head,
> I seen dis head ten thousand times befo'.

JESSIEE

I was reading to her, from this guidebook.
I was reading to her,
about the sunset luaus by the beach where you can learn to hula,
both boy hula and girl hula, and
I got hungry, just really really hungry.

KAHEKILI

> Jessiee!

JESSIEE

The surgery was going to be in a couple hours,

JESSIEE (cont)
Mom says I should go get something to eat,
that she would be fine for a while.

KAHEKILI
Jessiee!

JESSIEE
The surgery won't start for a couple hours.

KAHEKILI
I swim I swim I swim,
I stroke and stroke and stroke.

JESSIEE
So I went for a corndog.
Got in the car, drove down the road, looking for a sign, that said,

KAHEKILI
Jessiee!

JESSIEE
I don't know, corndog,

KAHEKILI
No head, no head, ocean bitch fuckin' eat her
up eat her up.

JESSIEE
And somehow I'm at the airport.

KAHEKILI
I look fo' da head, I know dis head,

JESSIEE
Found a sign, destination: Maui.

KAHEKILI
Seen dis head ten thousand times befo'.

JESSIEE
Not exactly corndog, but I felt like, that's where I might go, where I might –

KAHEKILI
I swim I swim I –

JESSIEE

Where I might fill my craving,

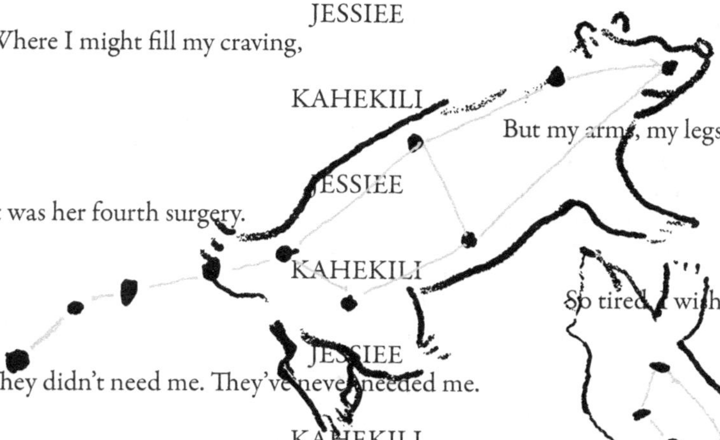

KAHEKILI

But my arms, my legs,

JESSIEE

It was her fourth surgery.

KAHEKILI

So tired, I wish,

JESSIEE

They didn't need me. They've never needed me.

KAHEKILI

I wish, still da watah stay!

JESSIEE

So I called Mom,
said Mom I'm going to Maui
She asked for some chocolate covered macadamia nuts,
I bought the ticket and jumped on the flight.

KAHEKILI

So I say, ocean you win.
I roll onto one small rock under da cliff.
I pick one star an' I pray to da buggah,
Please. Let Jessiee come to shore.

JESSIEE

Funny story, when I got that call, the only thing I could think about was, so, what do I do with all those chocolate covered macadamia nuts in my hotel room. I'm barely conscious in the water, and still I'm like, macadamia nuts.
I should give them to Kahekili. Or maybe he hates macadamia nuts.
Wow, I'm never gonna know if this kid liked macadamia nuts or not.

KAHEKILI

Den like a miracle,
psst psst blink blink,
da star show me,
Jessiee's head up an' down up an' down,
Jessiee's body over an' under da breaks,
I know right den, dat da shape odda body not breathing, an' no t'ink,
no plan a action,

> KAHEKILI (cont)
> I jus' fall straight back into dis watah again.

A loud splash, a body thrown into a mass of water.
Guidebook begins to underscore this moment with the previously
introduced Hawaiian Lullaby, while Kahekili embraces Jessiee
lifts her in his arms. Takes her to shore.
A long kiss. Like the first time they met.
And then the kiss turns into something else,
something more desperate.
When the song comes to the end of a verse:
Jessiee starts, chokes up water.

> KAHEKILI
> Kay den. You stay alright, stay alright,
> jus' spit all da ocean out, spit it out,
> Dass good, all a da ocean. Spit her out. Spit, kay den. Kay.

Kahekili collapses on the sand.
Lots of breathing. Breathing.

They lie there, staring up at the sky.

> JESSIEE
> Do you like macadamia nuts?

Kahekili shakes his head slowly.

> JESSIEE
> I'm leaving. Soon. Akron.
> I have these nuts, I don't need.
> I thought if you wanted them you could have them.

> KAHEKILI
> Jessiee,

> JESSIEE
> But you don't like them, which doesn't mean anything,

> KAHEKILI
> Jessiee.

> JESSIEE
> You can not like something and still have them.

KAHEKILI
Marry me.

JESSIEE
...

KAHEKILI
Marry me.

JESSIEE
...

KAHEKILI
Jessiee wid two ees, marry me.

JESSIEE
No.

KAHEKILI
I love you.

BOY
I love you.

JESSIEE
Not that simple.

KAHEKILI
Jus', I must live wid you fo'eva. Jus' I love you. Simple.

JESSIEE
You're young.
You don't understand what it means to have a life,

BOY
Do you?

KAHEKILI
I'm all buss up, Jessiee. I can't pingpong you right now.
Jus' I want fo' live wid you fo'eva. Don't leave. Easy.

BOY
We could run away? Like Robinson Crusoe.

JESSIEE
You are fifteen. I am thirty-two.

KAHEKILI
I look thirty-two. You look fifteen.
Without IDs, people t'ink I tek you on a ride, neh?

BOY
We could go to Hawaii.

KAHEKILI
Jessiee. You jus' fly off da cliff in da midnight.
I jus' wen save your life.
We can do anyt'ing. Jessiee, we can do any kine we want.

BOY
I could catch things in the sea, teach Jasmin how to hula,

KAHEKILI
Marry me.

JESSIEE
You are fifteen. I am thirty-two.

KAHEKILI
Da number of years lived on earth means
da number of years lived on earth.
Not'ing more. You trippin' over da kine sex.

JESSIEE
Kahekili.

KAHEKILI
No no, listen fo' me.
We had sex. But also we eat togedda, we have pingpong talk togedda, we get scared about each odda head be up down in da sea togedda, dass family,
Jessiee wid two ees, we already family, see?
We already married.

JESSIEE
You're good at this.

KAHEKILI
I'm good at a lot a t'ings. Marry me.

JESSIEE
I can't.

KAHEKILI
Because why!

JESSIEE
Because you are fifteen. And I'm, not.

The stars are many.

GUIDEBOOK *(As Airport PA)*
Passengers of US Airways Flight 17 bound for Cleveland with stops in Seattle and Atlanta, the departure gate has been changed to 30B. Also, there will be a slight delay to departure due to inclement weather. Thank you for your patience.

JESSIEE
Do you get people to see you off at the airport?
I don't. Sure, I get rides, I always have bundles of shit, But we get there, unload bags, then I send the driver on their way, outside the door.
Because, well,
it's awkward, isn't it?
You know one of you is going to go a very long way and it might be a while till you come back.
And those goodbyes, should be short and sweet. A hug and a peck.
Otherwise, it becomes an hour of staring at the crap coffee trying not to cry,
or an hour of talking about anything and everything trying to cram in every last bit of information about yourself into that other person's brain.
The crap thing is tho,
When you do successfully send the driver on their way, For some reason you still keep hoping,
maybe a miracle will happen,
and they will slide in through the gates,
out of breath and completely gross with sweat –
to plant that last final movie airport kiss,
cut to: few months later, they're married to you or something.

GUIDEBOOK *(As Airport PA—)*
Passengers of US Airways Flight 17 bound for Cleveland with stops in Seattle and Atlanta, the departure gate has been changed forever. Also, there will be an infinite delay to departure due to something or another. Stay a while, have a Mai Tai, get married and have babies, build a house, build a shrine of hands,

JESSIEE
They never do come back.
And it is because you sent them away.
And whether you believe you did the right thing or not, the law, the petitions, the picketlines, the shaking heads, the good-girl police in every well-meaning advice giver, crowds your choice with so much noise,
and you dare not ever voice what it meant,
what it cost you, to send them away, the way that you did.
Meanwhile, the fiction miracle loops on in your mind's movie.

KAHEKILI

Strange, fo' have some odda bugga in da head.
Strange, li'dat in your chest or some stuff.
Not pain, or li' "haaaak! I no can live no more!!"
but different.
Ocean smell different, rain fall different, food taste different,
An' I not even chop off my boob.
When Jessiee go, she wen' put da bags in da taxi,
an' give me one hug, quick kiss on da face,
and a whole lotta macadamia nuts.
I wen' turn around an' shoot straight da odda way.
Li'dat, straight da odda way.
I jus' wen' tek my board out to Honolua,
paddle some, nap some, look out at da sky some.
It's good.
I'm teaching myself to be jus' happy for her head be above watah, neh?
Maybe one day we gon' meet again,
maybe we don't,
but for today it's nice,
dat she mek me worry.

Seat belt on sign "ping."

A goodbye.

GUIDEBOOK

Mahalo, we hope you enjoyed your stay in Maui, Hawaii, one of the most sought after destinations on the planet. With over two and half million visitors almost every year, we know that you know that Maui is the most happiest place to be. Do come back.

End of Play

Acknowledgements

Thank you to every artist who have embedded their impact on the pages, margins and doodles of these three plays.
But for this collection specifically —
Thank you to —
Leigh Silverman, Dustin Wills, Julia Ritchey, Francis Jue, Paul Castles, Eze Jouley, Jihye Um, and Cexy Leuszler for your generous spirit, creative collaboration but mostly for your delightful gift of doodles.

Clint Ramos I want to print and frame your beautiful one line drawing of my face if I wasn't so embarrassed by how deeply narcissistic I am.

Sherla, Sarah, Jackie, Megan and the rest of Sledgehammer Series Team y'all are amazing. Tireless humans and I am honored and thrilled to be chosen as your first batch of what I hope is a long list of beautiful books of plays. ♥

tripwireharlot.com

www.ingramcontent.com/pod-product-compliance
Lightning Source LLC
Chambersburg PA
CBHW071229070526
44583CB00017B/2099